For Elissa Wein~

thanks, intues, work

JOHNNY TENORIO
AND OTHER PLAYS

Carlos Morton

Feb. 2014

Arte Publico Press
Houston
Texas
1992

Acknowledgements

This volume is made possible through a grant from the National Endowment for the Arts, a federal agency and the Ford Foundation.

The following people and institutions were instrumental in the development of this collection:
Webster Smalley, Theatre Department, University of Texas at Austin; Institute of Latin American Studies, U.T. Austin; Larry García, Teatro Toviah; Aztlán Cultural Center, San Antonio; Duo Theatre, New York; Romulus Zamora, Theatre Department, UCLA; The Group Theatre, Seattle; Cora Cardona, Teatro Dallas; Speech & Drama Department, Laredo Junior College; Joseph Papp, Oscar Ciccone, Cecilia Vega, Vicente Castro, New York Shakespeare Festival; Jorge Huerta, Teatro Ensemble de UCSD; Texas A&M University; Theatre Department, U.T. El Paso; Eduardo Rodríguez Solís, Programa Cultural de las Fronteras; Michael Birtwistle, Theatre & Dance, Amherst College; James Baldwin Playwriting Contest, UMAS Amherst; Bill Virchis; Theatre Department, The University of California, Riverside.

Arte Publico Press
University of Houston
Houston, Texas 77204-2090

Cover design by Mark Piñón

Johnny Tenorio & Other Plays/ Carlos Morton
    p.   cm.
    Contents: Johnny Tenorio — The savior — The miser of Mexico — Pancho Diablo.
    ISBN 1-55885-047-3
    1. Mexican Americans–Drama. I. Title. II. Title: Johnny Tenorio and other plays.
PS3563.O88194J64 1992
812'.54–dc20   91-40493
                                              CIP

The paper used in this publication meets the requirements of the American National Standard for Permanence of Paper for Printed Library Materials Z39.48-1984. ∞

A mi querida esposa Azalea Marín

Contents

Carlos Morton: Chicano Dramatist

It has been suggested that U.S. Hispanics will change the United States even as they are changed,[1] an idea which recalls José Vasconcelo's as yet unrealized dream of a new race. Currently in the U.S. we see evolving an era in which all races can contribute, share and benefit more than at any other time in our history. Certainly this is a harbinger of a future that is neither Anglo-American nor Hispanic, but rather a new miscegenation—*la raza cósmica* at last. Following futile efforts over the years to stem the flow of Hispanics into the U.S., and with the Hispanic denial of the value of assimilation now defunct, US/America will generally perceive the Latino presence to be less foreign. With the resulting lessened hostility, Hispanic Americans will more proudly offer their Latin American gifts in the long overdue process of miscegenation. Because we are in the early stages, however, there still remain real conflicts and real fears, but at least the process has begun. We have seen, for example, that while the U.S. Border Patrol works to stop illegal Hispanic immigrants, US/Americans stand in line for *La Bamba*; even as many clamor to make English the official language of the United States, Madonna and other singers record in Spanish.

An essential group in this transitional phase is the emerging cadre of Chicano playwrights whose voices are being heard by Anglos and Hispanics in off-Broadway plays and at many of the nation's foremost regional theatres—Manhattan's Public Theatre, the Milwaukee Repertory Theatre and the Los Angeles Theatre Center, as well as a number of smaller theatres, especially at universities across the U.S. Among these Chicano authors, and considered as one of the four outstanding younger Hispanic dramatists writing in the United States today,[2] is Carlos Morton.

Morton was born in 1947 in Chicago and, as the son of an Army-career father, traveled widely with his family, gaining experiences he would later use in his writing. After leaving home, Morton worked several years at odd jobs to support himself while working with various theatre groups such as The Second City and the San Francisco Mime Troupe. During these formative years, he also managed to obtain two university degrees. He later earned a Ph.D. in theatre at the University of Texas at Austin. During his colorful and varied career, Morton has written for television, taught speech and drama at several universities, contributed to publications in the U.S. and abroad, directed his own plays around the country, taught as a Fulbright Lecturer at the University of Mexico and published fiction, poetry and scholarly articles. His true calling, however, is that of dramatist. Once, responding to a question during an interview regarding writing plays, he remarked, "There is nothing else in the world I would rather do."[3] Morton now lives in Riverside, California where, in addition to his writing, he teaches drama at the Riverside campus of the University of California.

Morton has had his plays staged in numerous cities in the U.S. and has even begun to gain international exposure with the successful 1988 staging of his bilingual *Johnny Tenorio* in a European tour that included performances in Germany, France and Spain. This tour was followed by the more recent and also well-received performances of a Spanish version of the same play in Mexico City in 1989.[4]

Though he has been writing for some twenty years and is one of the most outstanding and successful contemporary Chicano dramatists, it has only been within the last several years that Carlos Morton's efforts have been widely recognized. As already mentioned, he received a Fulbright award for a year in Mexico, where he taught at the Centro de Enseñanza para Extranjeros at the Universidad Nacional Autónoma de México (1989–1990). In addition, he has published a series of play anthologies—*The Many Deaths of Danny Rosales and Other Plays* (1983), the current collection (1992), as well as a third collection of plays, translated into Spanish, which is scheduled for publication in Mexico under the title *Las muchas muertes de Danny Rosales y otras obras*. It is notable also that Morton's *El jardín* appears in a recent anthology of Texas plays.[5] Also to his credit are the numerous successful stagings of his works both here and abroad. Among some of the more important stagings of Morton's plays, we can cite *The Many Deaths of Danny Rosales* that won the Hispanic Playwrights Festival Award in 1986 in New York City, the production of *Pancho Diablo* in the New York Shakespeare Festival Latino in 1987, the summer 1988 stagings of *El jardín* in New York City by the Puerto Rican Traveling Theatre/El Teatro Rodante Puertorriqueño, the Denver Center Theatre's production of *Cuentos*, with Angel Vigil in 1988–89, and *Johnny Tenorio*, which, in addition to the European tour of 1988 mentioned earlier, has also been staged in Mexico City in 1989, and twice by the Teatro Dallas, in 1986 and 1990.

Morton continues to revise earlier plays as he writes new ones. Two examples of recently written pieces are the timely *At Risk*,

which deals with AIDS[6] and *The Miser of Mexico*, a *refundición* of
Moliere's famous play. The latter work was first staged in November 1989 at the University of Texas at El Paso, then again at
Amherst College in Massachusetts (1990), and most recently at
the University of California at Riverside (1991). Morton's current
theatrical project is a one-act play entitled *The Fatherless*, which
premiered in Dallas in the summer of 1991. The play is based on
a short story by Margarito Rodríguez that deals with the timely
problems of gangs in U.S. cities.

This anthology, *Johnny Tenorio and Other Plays*, includes four
successfully staged plays: *Johnny Tenorio* (1983), *The Savior*
(1986), *The Miser of Mexico* (1989) and *Pancho Diablo* (1987).

Johnny Tenorio

The first play in the collection, the highly successful *Johnny
Tenorio* (1983), is a contemporary manifestation of a long tradition
of adaptations of the Don Juan theme that was initiated in Spain
in 1630 with the publication of *El burlador de Sevilla* by Tirso
de Molina. With his Chicano Don Juan, Morton addresses the
Mexican-American problem of *donjuanismo* through the exciting
and universal figure of Don Juan. The Chicano in the audience
can readily and easily identify with Johnny, but Anglos also relate
to and enjoy the play. Almost any male—Hispanic or Anglo—can
empathize with a Don Juan. It has been pointed out, for example,
that "men can be divided into three classes—those who think they
are Don Juans, those who think they have been and those who
think they could have been but did not want to."[7] Female readers
can certainly relate to the theme, but I'm told by one of my female
colleagues that she is not sure that they can empathize with a Don
Juan.

Besides the prototypical Don Juan play by Tirso, and the almost
countless adaptations and versions from other European countries,
the Don Juan legend also has a long and deeply rooted tradition
on this side of the Atlantic. José Zorrilla's *Don Juan Tenorio* was
introduced on the Mexican stage in 1844; this play and various versions of it soon became, and continue to be, an integral part of the
annual celebration in Mexico of *El día de los muertos*. The Day
of the Dead tradition, although now losing some momentum in
Mexico, and while never being very important in the mainstream
United States culture, has nevertheless been maintained in the Chicano community. As an example, I would mention the Teatro Dallas' annual staging of a "Día de los muertos" piece. Their most re-

cent production, titled "An Evening With Don Juan" (October 18-
November 4, 1990), featured Morton's *Johnny Tenorio*.[8] I might
also cite another contemporary Don Juan play, *The Fabulous Life
and Death Adventures of Don Juan Tenorio*, by James Bierman.[9]

Although these Chicano plays are examples of Hispanic literature written in the United States, Morton's Don Juan play nevertheless has deep roots in Mexican culture. This is exemplified by,
among other things, the *corrido* entitled "Juan Charrasqueado," by
the Mexican composer Joaquín Cordero. It has been stated that
" ... to understand the Chicano, one needs to know not only Mexico and the Mexicans but also the Anglo. The Chicano is in many
ways a combination of the two cultures, or at least, the product of
the influences of the two."[10] This dualism can be seen in the play's
title, the author's name and background and the very important
Mexican ceremony of the Day of the Dead. In the competition between Johnny and his friend Louie to see who can seduce the most
women in one year, Johnny goes to the Anglo center of New York
City while Louie travels to Mexico City—the Mexican hub. Thus,
all through the play, and beginning with the first lines of *Johnny
Tenorio*, it is clear we are dealing with a Don Juan who lives and
loves in contemporary San Antonio, Texas, but who is influenced
by both New York and Mexico City. While Mexico's influence
on the Chicano is readily apparent, it should also be remembered
that the civilization of Mexico is undergirded by a powerful Indian
legacy—Aztec and Mayan among others.

It is well known that while Tirso's Don Juan is condemned to
Hell, Zorilla's romantic version allows Doña Inés to save him from
condemnation. Johnny Tenorio—unrepentant and with none of
his victims willing to forgive him—seems to complete the cycle by
being doomed to Hell, thereby sending a strong message to *machis-
tas* and Don Juans that reckless living with many *mamasotas* ends
in death and damnation. However, there exists at least one other
valid interpretation concerning Johnny's demise, and one that is
related to the Indian influence. This alternate conclusion, though
not sending Chicano *donjuanistas* a message, is certainly more pos-
itive for Tenorio. As we learn in the play, Big Berta's cantina is
Johnny's favorite haunt and the place to which he returns when
fatally wounded by a jealous husband. Berta, a cosmic bartender
and Johnny's friend and confidant, is also his Mother figure and
confessor as well as being a matronly *curandera*. Magician-like, she
creates for the audience a retrospective look at Johnny by means
of flashbacks.

Berta, however, can also be interpreted as the Aztec goddess

Coatlique—"la diosa de las inmundicias" and eater of the sins of man. It is Berta who has prepared Johnny's altar in the bar and given him the traditional meal of the Day of the Dead—*atole* and *tamales*, food that can as well be considered the communion. Following this line of reasoning, since Johnny has knelt before the altar of Berta/Coatlique and partaken of the communion offered, he is spared damnation. Therefore, we have a theory easy to accept when we consider that life and death in the Aztec vision of the world—symbolized as nine circles or cycles that represent the road to purification—provides one the way to return ultimately to the eternal present reincarnated as a hummingbird or some other object. In support of this theory, Gloria Calhoun writes that "Johnny regresará, no precisamente como un hombre, tal vez como un colibrí, una estrella, un árbol, etc. Los aztecas, panteístas, adoraban al sol, que es energía. ¿Cómo se puede matar la energía?"[11] This interpretation, although not intended by Morton, is not only interesting but also indicative of the richness of a play that permits several interpretations because it exists on different levels of reality.

Johnny Tenorio, then, is another example of the "gold" taken from what appears to be an inexhaustible mine—the Don Juan legend. Combined with the Day of the Dead ceremony, Morton's contemporary Chicano version of Don Juan achieves an interesting mix of universal literature and one of Mexico's oldest cultural traditions. This excellent example of bilingual Chicano theatre also provides an ideal vehicle for the dramatist to analyze two preoccupations—*machismo* and *donjuanismo*.

Pancho Diablo

When I think of *Pancho Diablo*, I always recall what I saw on the back of a truck once on a highway near Guadalajara, Mexico— "Pancho es como el diablo, no se ve pero existe." It may be true in Mexico, but never on the stage when Morton's *Pancho Diablo* plays. I still vividly recall watching a production of the musical comedy in August 1987 in New York City where the Devil existed and was very visible. *Pancho Diablo* (1987), Morton's first New York production, was written initially in 1974 and published in 1976 under the original title of *El cuento de Pancho Diablo*.[12] The play, described by Jorge Huerta as a "raucous comedy,"[13] is set in La Gran Cantina (Hell), Cielito Lindo (Heaven) and the Promised Land—Houston, Texas. *Pancho Diablo* is a continuation of another highly successful Morton play titled *El Jardín* (1973 and revised in 1989). In a conversation with God, in the last scene of

El Jardín, Serpiente (the Devil and later reincarnated as Pancho Diablo) confides that he is tired of his job, to which Dios replies: "Well, perhaps we can arrange a minor position for you in Purgatory ... "

The action of the sequel, *Pancho Diablo*, begins where *El Jardín* terminates. We learn quickly in the play that Pancho, after billions of years of managing Hell, is weary of his job. He needs to make a mid-life career change and approaches San Pedro concerning a new position and an audience with God to discuss the matter. San Pedro, however, is not very sympathetic to Pancho—he allows no meeting with God and at best offers him a "nice post in Purgatory" or a position in a branch office on the planet Pluto. Despite San Pedro's objections, the frustrated Pancho decides to leave the cantina, anyway. Removing his horns and tail, Pancho leaves the "hell of the Chicano," singing "Adiós cabrones," and crosses the river as an *espalda mojada* in search of a better life in Texas.

The remainder of the play deals with Pancho's slow evolution toward becoming a more human-like and less devilish being. Pancho begins the slow but sure process as the proprietor of "Pancho's Palacio"—a chain of funeral parlors—when he decides to use the assets of the lucrative business to do good on Earth. The *diablos*, defeated by the women in the battle of the sexes in La Gran Cantina, follow Pancho to Earth but with no good intentions. They represent evil, while Pancho acquires a conscience and thus good and evil vie for control of the protagonist.

Near the end of the play it is learned that both the U.S. and the Soviet Union have launched pre-emptive strikes and total destruction of the planet is eminent. Meanwhile, Dios has disguised himself as a border patrol officer and he and Pancho have a battle that symbolizes the eternal struggle between good and evil. In short order, God wins, disarms the missiles, brings Pancho back to life and grants his request to continue on Earth. Thus, the victorious and forgiving Dios is now viewed as more human-like and is a hero to the popular masses. In the last lines of the play, God agrees that if Super Chuy (God's son Jesus) and San Pedro will take care of matters in Heaven during his absence, he will spend the next hundred years on Earth with his favorite creation—the earthlings.

Having the Devil operate a funeral parlor, God disguised as a border patrolman and Jesus living on Cloud Nine still suffering from the trauma of the crucifixion after two-thousand years are to be expected in Morton's theatre. A common trait of his characters is their unorthodox portrayal and the frequent depiction of epic and mythical personages as ordinary humans.

In the course of the play, then, Morton manages, among many other things, to attack *machismo*, the shortcomings of the Church and those who try to deny their Hispanic heritage. Thus, he creates Mary the bartender who ultimately removes her blonde wig and announces that she is María Nochebuena and proud of it! To conclude, it must be said that on stage *Pancho Diablo* is two hours of theatrical fun with a message, a lot of comedy and much food for thought.

The Miser of Mexico

The Miser of Mexico (1989), originally titled *The Miser of Monterrey*, is a *refundición* of Moliere's classic play. Morton readily admits that his theatrical piece is freely adapted from Moliere, but reminds us that the French playwright also borrowed heavily from Plautus to create his work. Morton's miser play is set in northern Mexico just prior to the Revolution of 1910, and Don Profundo, the miser, is modeled after the historic minister of finance under Porfirio Díaz—Don José Ives Limatour. *The Miser of Mexico* depicts a family consisting of the main character Don Profundo Quequemáfer (nicknamed Cacamáfer by his servants), his son Clemente (madly in love with the maid Mariana, who the miser plans to marry), and the daughter Elisa who is in love with Valentín de la Sierra, who had earlier saved her from Apache Indians in the desert of Chihuahua. Valentín, for his brave actions, is consequently rewarded by the miser by making him his mayordomo. The miser, however, has other marriage plans for Elisa. The complication here is that the pairings of Clemente/Mariana and Elisa/Valentín are socially inappropriate relationships in Mexican society of the time. The play, then, is about love and greed, but also it treats *mestizaje*, revolution and gender. Another character is Valentín's brother, Pancho Pérez, who is in the mountains awaiting the start of the Revolution. Additionally, in the miser's household we find Clemente's servant Filero and Tan-Tan who serves Don Profundo as valet, cook, coachman, waiter and butler. Other characters include Maruja, the maid and lover of Filero, Mariana's aunt Fanny and a frequent visitor of the Casa Grande—the wealthy crony of the miser—Generalísimo Rabioso Resbaloso. The miser plans to marry off his daughter Elisa to Resbaloso because he has agreed to take her without a dowry.

Morton has chosen, in his version of the miser play, to reduce some of Moliere's roles while keeping his characterizations and adding different plot elements. One important difference is that Moliere's miser gets his money back, while in Morton's version he doesn't. In *The Miser of Mexico*, servants hide Don Profundo's money in a *piñata* and later Pancho Pérez (a revolutionary reminiscent of Pancho Villa) fires his pistol in the air near the end of the play and a stray bullet strikes the money-filled *piñata*, allowing the servants to gather the falling money.

It seems at this point that the play will have a happy conclusion; but nevertheless, the ending is unexpectedly tragic. As mariachi music plays and bottles of tequila are passed around, trouble begins. Pancho, Clemente and Valentín begin a serious conversation. Valentín, supporting Clemente's idea of organizing a constitutional convention, tells Pancho that Mexico has to start talking and stop shooting. A heated discussion between Pancho and Clemente ends when the former arrests his little brother for counter-revolutionary activity. As Pancho and Clemente leave the stage, Valentín, at the insistence of Mariana, pulls his pistol and a shot rings out off stage. During this moment of mystery, chaos and confusion— Quequemáfer looks very old and vulnerable as the lights slowly fade.

The Savior

A prize-winning play,[15] *The Savior* (1986) treats the death, and the period just prior to it, of Archbishop Oscar Romero el El Salvador. In this two-act play we find, as in *Johnny Tenorio*, the use of flashbacks. Both Johnny and the Archbishop Romero are dead when the play begins and they participate only during the flashbacks. Both men die violently, Johnny by a knife and the Archbishop by a sniper's bullet. This, however, is where the similarities end. A notable difference between the two plays is that in *Johnny Tenorio* both Johnny and the reader/spectator finally come to the realization that he is dead while in *The Savior*, the nearer the end of the play the reader/spectator gets, the more alive Romero becomes, both in appearance on the stage and in the hearts of the audience or the people of El Salvador. At the end of the play we see that Romero, the Savior, has been resurrected and lives anew and forever in the minds and hearts of his flock.

The Savior begins on Palm Sunday, March 30, 1980 in the main cathedral of San Salvador—six days after Oscar Romero was shot dead. Morton, before writing this play, and a common practice with him, researched fully the topic before beginning to write. Morton devoted five years of research to the project and made two trips to Central America to interview people who knew Romero. During this process, and even initially, when first attracted to write a play about the barbaric assassination of the Archbishop, Morton began to find parallels between Romero and Jesus Christ—thus the title of the drama. It is interesting to note that shortly after beginning to write *The Savior*, Morton suffered from a mental block and was unable to continue the project. He then began to listen to the taped interviews he had made in El Salvador of those who had known Romero personally. Morton was so inspired by the oral accounts of the people who had witnessed the passion, struggle and agony of the Archbishop (who had given his life for them) that he was able to finish the play.

In *The Savior*, the reader/spectator gets a cross-sectional view of contemporary El Salvadoran society and of all the country's problems—the military controlled government with its soldiers and death squads, the Church, the rebels and the innocent and victimized *campesinos*, along with a number of *calaveras*. Morton points out that "Archetypical characters can be more calavera-like than those who are realistically drawn." Also we find the meddling US/American reporter and the U.S. Ambassador. Although most characters have names, they are usually designated as Campesina, Soldado, Presidente and Oligarchy. This allegorical value suggests a more general mood and that the problems facing El Salvador are those of all levels of society. The *calaveras* have been used to underscore that El Salvador is in the throes of a civil war and everyone is dying—from battle, poverty and starvation. Also, and in addition to physical death, there is spiritual death (the clergy) and there are those who are intellectually dead (the U.S. Ambassador). Also, a *calavera* can become a different character simply by changing hats. This allows one actor to play several roles. It is notable that Romero is the only personage of the cast who is not a *calavera*.

The play is political and the reader/spectator readily perceives the conflicts associated with the interventionist policies of the United States: at one point the U.S. Ambassador offers Romero money and encourages him to leave the country. On another occasion Oligarchy says to the Ambassador, "When Washington barks, he jumps," and a short time later the Ambassador says to Oligarchy, "Don't you think your next president should be a civilian, a democrat, elected by the people?" Actual slogans such as "Be a Patriot, Kill a Priest!—White Warriors Union" are found in the play along with comments made by the Death Squads like—"Our struggle is not against the Church but against the Jesuit guerrillas." The Death Squad reads a War Order that states that all Jesuits must leave El Salvador within 30 days or by July 20, 1977, and eventu-

ally executes Father Grande, the altar boy and an old man in the
cathedral.

The Savior can be classified as a docudrama reminiscent of Morton's *The Many Deaths of Danny Rosales*; however, Morton uses
parody and fantasy that allow the Romero play to become something much more complex. For example, in one scene we find
Romero in Rome during a flashback where, after a meeting with
the Pope, he is tempted in a way that recalls the temptation of
Christ in the desert. It is notable that in yet another scene there
is a grotesque parody of the Last Supper that involves the Death
Squad composed of Alvarez, Oligarchy and Presidente. Here the
wine and the wafer is a cup of blood and a piece of raw meat.
The tempter accuses and taunts Romero as do three bishops who
appear as apparitions. Romero is able to resist the Tempter who
ultimately changes from his original appearance as a kindly old
man to what he really is, the Devil. Defeated in his efforts, the
Devil then disappears.

As mentioned earlier, the reader/spectator can witness the
steady evolution of a Romero who changes both physically and
spiritually as he becomes more Christ-like. As Jesus died so that
His believers might have everlasting life, so Romero dies in order
to save the people of El Salvador. Romero, at the conclusion of
the play, is very much alive and enters symbolically from the audience. As the people gather around the resurrected Romero, those
who "killed" him—the president, the bishop, Oligarchy and the
US/American Ambassador suggestively exit.

In the remainder of this study we will consider some of the
aspects of Morton's dramaturgy that account, at least in part, for
his popularity and importance as a Chicano playwright. Morton
is one of the busiest of the contemporary Chicano playwrights and
all of his plays written to date have been staged—making him one
of the most produced of all the Chicano dramatists. Two of his
plays, *At Risk* and *The Foundling*, are also available on video.

Despite varying widely in form and subject, Morton's plays lend
themselves to grouping. *Johnny Tenorio* is based on the legend of
Don Juan and the Mexican Day of the Dead; *Pancho Diablo* (along
with *El Jardín*) is based on Christian myth; *The Miser of Mexico* is
based on Mexican and Mexican-American myth and history; and
The Savior (as is *The Many Deaths of Danny Rosales*) is based on
contemporary events. With the exception of *Johnny Tenorio*, the
three other plays of this collection have a very definite political

tone. Also, religion (Catholicism) has at least a minor role in each of the four plays.

It has been noted elsewhere that the strength of Morton's work lies in "his fresh blending of wide ranging and often exotic materials as well as his sense of commitment (Martin, 272)." Once, during an interview with Morton in Mexico City regarding his fresh approach to old themes, he remarked, " ... a veces hay variaciones nuevas y es ésta una razón por la atracción de *Johnny*. Es un Don Juan por otros ojos, es decir, de otra perspectiva."[16]

One of the more striking characteristics of Morton's work is that while most of his plays are comical (they are funny when read and during performances audiences laugh), there is always present a serious undertone. Perhaps a better way of saying this is that the play's entertainment value also has substance. This style is a result, at least in part, of Morton's stated criteria of the essential characteristics of good drama—"A play should educate and entertain."[14] Considering strictly the plays contained in this anthology, only *The Savior* is predominantly serious, although even this play, that deals with the grave matter of the assassination of Archbishop Romero, has its humor. For example, in a scene where a reporter interviews the president of El Salvador, the head of the country makes the University of Texas "Hook 'em horns" sign and the droll humor is underscored when he actually shouts "Hook 'em horns!" This outlandish style of humor is also seen in *Pancho Diablo* as exemplified by the comment made by the lady bartender Mary Goodnight, who says to God (disguised as a border patrolman) when he asks for another beer, "Jeeez! Haven't you had enough? You drank seventeen cases already!" This type of humor is further illustrated in *The Miser of Mexico* when Don Profundo says, in a conversation with his son Clemente, "I even found that she is of noble blood—partly. On her mother's stepsister's side she is a cousin twice removed of Hernan Cortés' sergeant-at-arms!" Finally, in *Johnny Tenorio* we find, "Vas a ser el primer astronauta que come tacos en el espacio," and in the same play in the scene with the lists of seduced women, the audience laughs when a large stack of computer printout paper is brought forth and unfolded to substantiate Johnny's claims of conquests.

Morton tends to adapt universal themes, myths and personages "a la chicana" in order to utilize them to address the needs of the Chicano community. The Devil, Don Juan, Jesus Christ, God and the Garden of Eden are examples of such practice. The Devil and God figure importantly in *Pancho Diablo* and *El Jardín* (not included in this anthology), and Archbishop Romero in *The Savior* is depicted as a Christ-like figure. Also, in each instance the deity is portrayed as a human-like figure who is also obviously Chicano. The plays are often set in Heaven, Hell and Earth and specifically in Texas when the drama takes place on Earth. Texas, for example, is the setting of both *Johnny Tenorio* and *Pancho Diablo*, and though *The Miser of Mexico* is set in northern Mexico, the scant information concerning the setting places the scene of action in or near Juárez, and right across the border from El Paso, Texas.

The adaptation of unrelated topics to the needs of the Chicano is associated with Morton's penchant for writing *refundiciones* of other plays, that is: his "a la chicana" adaptations of universal and mythical figures. In this anthology, we find *Johnny Tenorio*, a Chicano Don Juan, and *The Miser of Mexico*, a Mexican/Chicano version of the famous miser of Moliere. Although not included in the present collection, we should also mention Morton's *Malinche*, a play fashioned after Euripides' *Medea* and influenced by Gorostiza's *La Malinche* (1958).

A consideration of character portrayal in Morton's plays is yet another way to approach an appreciation of his dramaturgy. Anyone not accustomed to the typical Morton character might at first be somewhat taken aback, but the reader/spectator soon becomes used to such character portrayals as a Jesus called Super Chuy living on Cloud Nine still suffering from the trauma of the crucifixion, or a God depicted with a Zapata mustache coming to Earth disguised as the *migra*, or even a Devil called Pancho who, ready for a mid-life career change, leaves Hell and swims the Rio Grande as a wetback on his way to a better life in Houston, Texas, where he founds the world's largest fast-funeral parlor franchise "ofreciendo entierros to go." And there is Johnny Tenorio, a Chicano version of Don Juan, as expressed in his speech, his dress and his adventures in New York City and San Antonio, Texas. Regardless of whether one reads the play script or views a production of it, Johnny is obviously a Don Juan, and equally obvious, he is Chicano.

Finally, and although not included in the present collection, a brief consideration of *El Jardín* is warranted for several reasons. First, *Pancho Diablo* is a sequel of *El Jardín* and bears out much of what has been said thus far concerning the Carlos Morton plays in general. *El Jardín* is also typical of Morton's earlier plays that are in contrast to his more mature work contained in this anthology. In a scene in which the Devil is tempting Eve to taste the apple, or rather the *tuna*, he strives to impress her with his ability to see into the future and gives Eve a vision of what will transpire later in history. He points out the planet Earth below and asks Eve to

blow away the clouds, consequently revealing Columbus and Bo-
rinquen the Taíno. Time thus flashes forward to 1492, and what
follows is a very curious and comical scene that depicts the ini-
tial meeting of Europe and America. The scene is strange in that
time periods are jumbled—Columbus decides to settle the New
World, to put in freeways from Corpus Christi to San Francisco
and to construct Taco Bells boasting distinct Spanish architecture,
while Taíno learns to speak Spanish all within the space of a few
lines. The rest of the scene gives us a quick but disordered review of the history of the Americas and the injustices committed
by the Europeans. For their services, for example, the Indians are
promised five coconuts a day, whisky, gin and smallpox. In re-
gard to *El Jardín* specifically, it is of note that an article in *Time*
magazine categorizes Morton's work as mingling "reality and daffy
fantasy, human characters and cartoonish stereotypes in order to
teach—or preach—the Hispanic history of the Americas" (82–83).
While this assessment is accurate to a minor degree for most of
Morton's plays, it is more applicable to Morton's early plays, such
as *Los dorados* and *Rancho Hollywood*. It has very limited appli-
cability to plays like *Johnny Tenorio, Pancho Diablo, The Savior
and The Miser of Mexico*, all of which are included in this volume.
The most accurate part of the statement is that Morton intends to
teach. He does so by using epic figures like Don Juan and the Devil,
more contemporary heroes such as Oscar Romero and timely is-
sues like AIDS and the ever-growing problem of inner-city gangs.
He uses fantasy and humor to convey his message. He not only
wants to educate but to entertain as well. Finally, the works contained in this collection exemplify the latest of Morton's theatrical
efforts and are representative of some of his best work. Whether
one reads a given piece only, or has the opportunity to see it on
stage, one will not soon forget a play by Carlos Morton—one of
the pre-eminent Chicano dramatists of the late twentieth century.

Lee A. Daniel
Texas Christian University

Notes

[1]Rodríguez, Richard. "The Fear of Losing a Culture." *Time*
(July 11, 1988), 84.
[2]Henry, William A. "Visions From the Past: Emerging Playwrights Trade Anger for Dialogue." *Time* (July 11, 1988), 82.

³Daniel, Lee A. "An Interview with Carlos Morton," *Latin American Theatre Review* 23/1 (Fall 1989), 144.

⁴_____ , "Un pocho en México—una entrevista con Carlos Morton." An interview done March 1990 in Mexico City. Forthcoming in *Confluencia*.

⁵Martin, William B. *Texas Plays*. (Dallas: Southern Methodist University Press, 1990), 167–197.

⁶*At Risk* has been staged successfully several times and has also been video-taped and is available for purchase. There is additionally a comic book version of the play obtainable in English and Spanish.

⁷Feal, Carlos. *En nombre de Don Juan (Estructura de un mito literario)*. Amsterdam: John Benjamins, 1988, 1.

⁸Daniel, Lee A. "An Evening With Don Juan" in the "Plays in Performance" section of the *Latin American Theatre Review* 24/2 (Spring 1991), 164–166.

⁹Bierman, James. A summary and discussion of the work is found in the "Plays in Performance" section of the *Latin American Theatre Review*, 18/1 (Fall 1984), 131–135.

¹⁰Daniel, Lee A. "*Johnny Tenorio: Don Juan a la Chicana*," *Confluencia*, Fall 1989, 80.

¹¹A personal letter to me from Gloria Calhoun dated November 11, 1990.

¹²Huerta, Jorge A. *Chicano Theatre: Themes and Forms*. Ypsilanti, Mich.: Bilingual Press/Editorial Bilingüe, 1982.

¹³Huerta, *Chicano Theatre: Themes and Forms*, 168.

¹⁴Daniel, *Latin American Theatre Review*, 146.

¹⁵*The Savior* won second prize in the James Baldwin Playwriting Contest, Amherst College, 1990.

¹⁶Daniel, "Un pocho en México," (See number 4 above).

PLAYS BY CARLOS MORTON

1. *Desolation Car Lot* (1971)—a one-act play.

2. *El Jardín* (1989)—a one-act play. First published in *El Grito* in 1974.

3. *Pancho Diablo* (1987)—a two-act play. Originally titled *El cuento de Pancho Diablo* (1976).

4. *The Many Deaths of Danny Rosales** (1974, 1986)—a two-act play.

5. *Lilith* (1977)—a one-act play. (Although the play has been performed, Morton considers it a play in progress.)

6. *Los Dorados* (1978)—a one-act play.

7. *Rancho Hollywood* (1979)—a two-act play.

8. *Squash* (in collaboration with the San Francisco Mime Troupe) (1979)—a one-act play.

9. *Johnny Tenorio* (1983)—a one-act play.

10. *Malinche* (1984)—a one-act play.

11. *The Savior* (1986)—a two-act play.

12. *Cuentos* (1987) (with Angel Vigil)—a one-act play.

13. *The Foundling* (1988)—a two-act play. A video version is available of this play.

14. *At Risk* (1989)—a one-act play. A video version is available of this play. Published also as a comic book.

15. *The Miser of Mexico* (1989)—a two-act play.†

16. *The Dropout* (1990)—a one-act play.

17. *The Fatherless* (1991)—a one-act play.

---

*The title of this play has changed, depending on the various versions of its evolution. The first title used was *Las Many Muertes de Richard Morales* (published in *Tejidos* in 1977), *Las muchas muertes de Richard Morales* (published in *Conjunto* in 1980), *Las muchas muertes de Danny Rosales* (to be published in Mexico) and the title listed above in number one that was published in the first Arte Publico collection (1983).

†In this list of works, 11 are one-act pieces and six are two-act plays. Morton's plays have been produced in Texas, California, New York, Iowa, Minnesota, Colorado, Washington, and New Mexico. Countries where Morton's theatrical pieces have been staged abroad: France, Germany, Mexico and Spain.

SELECTED STUDIES
TREATING CARLOS MORTON'S THEATRE

ARTICLES

Daniel, Lee A. "An Interview With Carlos Morton," *Latin American Theatre Review*, 23/1 (Fall 1989), 143–150.

———— . *"Johnny Tenorio*: Don Juan a la Chicana," *Confluencia*, Fall 1989, 79–83.

Pross, Edith. "A Chicano Play and its Audience." *The Americas Review* 14 (Spring 1986), 71–79.

REVIEWS

a.) Newspapers

Morton's plays have been reviewed in newspapers across the nation ranging from university papers to the *New York Times* and are too numerous to mention. Play reviews have also been published in newspapers in Mexico, France and Germany.

b.) Journals

Aparicio, Frances R. *Nuevos Pasos: Chicano and Puerto Rican Drama, Hispania* 73, December 1990, 1001–1002. Review of *Rancho Hollywood*.)

Bruce-Novoa, Juan. *Nuevos Pasos: Chicano and Puerto Rican Drama, Latin American Theatre Review*, 14/1 (Fall 1980), 108–110. (Review of *Rancho Hollywood*.)

Daniel, Lee A. "An Evening With Don Juan," *Latin American Theatre Review*, 24/2 (Spring 1991), 164–166. (Review of *Johnny Tenorio*.)

Gonzales-Berry, Erlinda. *Latin American Theatre Review*, (Spring 1989), 132–133. (Review of *The Many Deaths of Danny Rosales and Other Plays* that contains *The Many Deaths of Danny Rosales, Rancho Hollywood, Los Dorados* and *El Jardín*.)

McCaffrey, Mark. "Los dorados," *Latin American Theatre Review* 12/1 (Fall 1978), 89–90.

McClellan, Bennett. "Performance Review: *El Garden*," *Latin American Theatre Review* 10/2 (Spring 1977), 77–79.

BOOKS AND MAJOR STUDIES
THAT INCLUDE MORTON'S WORK

Huerta, Jorge. *Chicano Theatre: Themes and Forms.* Ypsilanti, Michigan: Bilingual Press/Editorial Bilingüe, 1982.

Rocard, Marcienne. "Les Fils Du Soleil: La minorité Mexicaine à Travers la Littérature des Etats-Unis," Paris.

Tatum, Charles. *Chicano Literature.* Boston: Twayne Publishers, 1982.

MASTER'S THESIS

Arrizón, María Alicia. "Estrategias Dramáticas en la obra de Carlos Morton Pérez." Master's thesis, Arizona State University, 1986. Arrizón treats the following plays: *Rancho Hollywood, El Jardín* and *Johnny Tenorio.*

ANTHOLOGIES

1. Morton, Carlos. *The Many Deaths of Danny Rosales, and Other Plays.* Houston, Texas: Arte Publico Press, 1983. (This collection contains *The Many Deaths of Danny Rosales, Rancho Hollywood, Los Dorados* and *El Jardín.*) These plays are bilingual and written predominantly in English.

2. _____ . *Johnny Tenorio and Other Plays.* Houston, Texas: Arte Publico Press, 1992. (This collection contains *Johnny Tenorio, The Savior, The Miser of Mexico,* and *Pancho Diablo.*) *The Savior* and *The Miser of Mexico* are published here for the first time.

3. Villanueva, Tino. Editor, *Chicanos: Antología histórica y literaria.* México: Fondo de Cultura Económica, 1980. (Contains *El Jardín.*)

4. Kanellos, Nicolás y Jorge A. Huerta, editores, *Nuevos Pasos: Chicano and Puerto Rican Drama.* Houston, Texas: Arte Publico Press, 1979 and 1989. (Contains *Rancho Hollywood.*)

5. Martin, William B., editor, *Texas Plays.* Dallas: Southern Methodist University Press, 1990. (Contains *El Jardín.*)

Johnny Tenorio

CHARACTERS

JOHNNY TENORIO, twenties, a lady-killer.
BIG BERTA, earthmother, curandera of indeterminate age.
DON JUAN, Johnny's father, fiftysh.
LOUIE MEJÍA, twenties, a would be lady-killer.
ANA MEJÍA, Johnny's novia, Louie's sister. Late teens.

The scene is Big Berta's Bar on the West Side of San Antonio, Texas. At center is a wooden bar with barstools. Atop the bar is an elaborate "altar," the kind used in Mexico during the "Day of the Dead" ceremonies. On one side of the bar, high above the liquor bottles, is a painting of La Virgen de Guadalupe. The bar has the feeling of an arena, with saw dust on the floor—the better to soak up the blood and spittle. Some tables with chairs are interspersed throughout. A gaudy jukebox is in one corner. There is also a front door leading to the outside. Enter BERTA to sing "El Corrido de Juan Charrasqueado."

BERTA: Voy a cantarles un corrido muy mentado. Lo que ha pasado en la hacienda de la flor. (_Enter_ JOHNNY _miming the galloping and bucking of a "horse."_)

    La triste historia de un ranchero enamorado. (_Echando gritos._)
    Que fue borracho, parrandero y jugador
    Juan se llamaba y lo apodaban Charrasqueado,

(JOHNNY _tips his sombrero, reins in, and parks his steed._)

    Era valiente y arriesgado en el amor.
    A las mujeres más bonitas se llevaba.
    En aquellos campos no quedaba ni una flor.

(_Enter_ ANA, _playing the coquette—also wearing calavera mask. Tempo slows._)

JOHNNY: (_Passionately, he snatches up_ ANA _into his arms._) ¡Véngase conmigo, Mamasota!
ANA: (_Barely protesting._) !Ay, Señor! ¡Déjeme! ¡Soy Señorita, y estoy prometida!
JOHNNY: ¡Así me gustan más! (_Carrying_ ANA _shrieking and kicking offstage._)
BERTA: Un día domingo que se andaba emborrachando. (_Enter_ JOHNNY _with a bottle of tequila._)

    A la cantina le corrieron a avisar
    Cuídate, Juan, que por ahí te andan buscando.
    Son muchos hombres, no te vayan a matar.

JOHNNY: Pues, que se pongan, ¡a ver quién es el más macho! (_Enter_ LOUIE _with calavera mask and gun drawn._)
BERTA: No tuvo tiempo de montar a su caballo. (_Slow motion:_ JOHNNY _mounts his horse as he is shot by_ LOUIE.)

Pistola en mano se lo echaron de un montón.

JOHNNY: Ando borracho (*Beat.*) y son buen gallo.

BERTA: ¡Cuando una bala atravesó su corazón! (JOHNNY *falls in a heap on the floor as* LOUIE *exits. Two beats.* JOHNNY *sits up abruptly and looks at audience.*)

JOHNNY: ¡Ajúa! (*Letting loose a grito and rising to his feet.*) A mí no me matan tan fácil, ¡cabrones! (*He exits laughing and swaggering.* BERTA *commences to wipe the bar, whistling the corrido as though nothing had happened.*)

DON JUAN: (*Entering bar.*) Berta! Are you open?

BERTA: Claro que sí, pásele, pásele, Don Juan. I was playing one of my favorite rancheritas.

DON JUAN: (*Motioning to the altar.*) ¡Mira no más!

BERTA: You like it?

DON JUAN: ¡Qué emoción!

BERTA: Pues, ya sabe. Hoy es el Día de los Muertos y tonight the souls return to their favorite hangouts. Are you ready?

DON JUAN: Sí, traje mi máscara. (*Showing* BERTA *a calavera mask.*)

BERTA: Wonderful. There will be velorios and speeches expressing el amor and esteem que sentimos por ellos. ¡Esta noche, Don Juan, celebramos a La Muerte! (*Pouring him a tequila.*)

DON JUAN: Pues como dicen los gringos—"I'll drink to that." (*Raising his glass.*)

BERTA: ¡A las almas perdidas! (*They click glasses, drink it in one gulp, and wash it down with slices of lime.*) Ahora, a ver si puedes adivinar—who's altar is that?

DON JUAN: A ver, a ver, a ver. ¡No me digas!

BERTA: Yes, he liked to gamble. (*Holding up the dice.*) And he liked tequila.

DON JUAN: ¡También! (BERTA *shows* DON JUAN *the centerfold of a Playboy magazine.*) He died of this!

DON JUAN: ¡A Chihuahua! ¡Ya sé de quién es!

BERTA: (*Holding up a list.*) Watcha, a list of his conquistas— ¿Quieres oírlas?

DON JUAN: No, no, no. (*Visibly shaken.*)

BERTA: You've got to hear this. (BERTA *reads list.*)

In Texas, six hundred and forty.
Arizona, two hundred and thirty.
California, one hundred, and look,
New York, already one thousand!

Among them you'll find
camareras, cantineras
farmer's daughters, city girls
abogadas, tamaleras
there are women of every grade
every form, every stage.

To him all blondes are sexy
Asian women, quite perplexing
English gals are domineering
and Latinas so endearing.

In winter he likes gorditas
in summer, he likes flaquitas
he finds the tall ones challenging
the short ones are always charming.

He'll seduce an older dama
just to add her to his list
and he'll tell the younger girls
"m'hija, you don't know what you've missed!"

He cares not, be they ricas
be they ugly, be they chicas
as long as it's a skirt
he is there to chase and flirt.

DON JUAN: ¡Madre de Dios!

BERTA: Ruega por nosotros.

DON JUAN: (*Crossing himself.*) Y por el alma del difunto.

BERTA: Y sabes que, after every conquest, every amorío, he would
come here a confesarse, to cleanse himself. Big Berta's Bar
was his fuente de la juventud. (*A loud knocking is heard at
the front door.*) Who's there? (*Walking over to the door.*)
We're closed! (*Knocking continues, louder now.*) Pinches
borrachos, cómo friegan. (*Looking through the peephole.*)
¡Es él!

DON JUAN: ¿Quién?

BERTA: ¡El Johnny!

DON JUAN: ¿Juanito?

BERTA: He's early, no lo esperaba hasta medianoche. Ponte tu
máscara, I don't want him to recognize you. (DON JUAN
goes and sits on a bar stool as BERTA *goes to open the door
to let* JOHNNY *in.*)

JOHNNY: (*Staggering in, his face a deathly pale.*) Berta! Tequila! (JOHNNY *sits down slowly, painfully.*)

BERTA: Coming right up. (*She goes behind bar to serve him.*)

JOHNNY: (*To* DON JUAN.) What you doing, playing trick or treat? (DON JUAN *turns his gaze away and lowers his head in grief.*) Weird customers you got here, Berta.

BERTA: (*Serving* JOHNNY.) ¿Qué te pasa, Johnny? Your hands are shaking, you're white as a ghost. And what's this on your shirt, sangre?

JOHNNY: I got in a fight with a jealous husband. ¡Pinche gringo!

BERTA: ¡Otra vez el burro al trigo! What happened?

JOHNNY: ¿Qué crees? (*Pulls out his gun and lays it on the table.*) Blam, blam, blam. Laid him low. Bloody scene, wife screaming hysterically over the body. Police sirens.

BERTA: Ay, Johnny, ¿Por qué te metes siempre en tantos líos?

JOHNNY: (*Patting* BERTA *on the ass.*) I like to live dangerously.

BERTA: (*Slaps his hand hard.*) Johnny, Johnny, let me clean your wounds.

JOHNNY: No problem, Berta, no problem. Just a minor little flesh wound. So, where's all the batos locos?

BERTA: (*Picking up his gun and laying it on the altar.*) No te apures, they'll be around later.

JOHNNY: I haven't been here since ...

BERTA: Since you stabbed Louie Mejía con un filero right here. (*Pointing to a spot on the floor.*)

JOHNNY: Ay, Berta, you don't have to brag about my exploits.

DON JUAN: ¿Mató a un hombre allí?

JOHNNY: You can almost see the blood stains on the floor.

DON JUAN: Pero, ¿cómo, por qué?

JOHNNY: Because I felt like it.

DON JUAN: ¡Qué lástima!

JOHNNY: Hey, well, it was him or me. Law of the jungle. Snarl, growl.

DON JUAN: ¡Qué lástima! ¡Que Dios te perdone!

JOHNNY: Hey, look, Pop, I don't need nobody's pardon. Besides, what's it to you, anyway? (*Walking over to* DON JUAN.)

BERTA: (*Stopping him.*) Never mind, Johnny, he's just a customer. Toma, otro tequila, on the house. (*She pours him another tequila.*)

JOHNNY: (*Grabbing* BERTA *by the waist and sitting her on his lap.*) Hey, Berta, why don't you marry me, huh?

BERTA: Johnny, you're not my type. Además, coqueteas con todas las rucas—how do I know you'll be true to me?

JOHNNY: Berta, you're my main squeeze. I'd die for you, you know that. (*Trying to kiss her passionately on the lips,* BERTA *disengages. It is a game they always play.*)

BERTA: Johnny, ¿sabes qué día es?

JOHNNY: I don't know, Saturday? It's always Saturday night for me.

BERTA: Johnny, hoy es El Día de los Muertos. Que si te digo que tengo el poder de hacer las almas aparecer. Think I can do it?

JOHNNY: (*Going along with it.*) Of course, you're a curandera.

BERTA: Muy bien, Johnny. Close your eyes, concentrate real hard. (*A flute, high and erie sounds in the distance.*) ¡Escucha! ¿Oyes algo? (*Drum beats.*) These are the sounds of the past, Johnny, sonidos de nuestros antepasados.

JOHNNY: Yeah, I can dig it—Halloween.

BERTA: (*Drums and flutes sound louder. All flashbacks proceeded by this method.*) ¡Qué Halloweenie ni qué mi abuela! I'm talking about Mictla, the underworld, the place where the bones rest. Y aquí llega la primera visita, Johnny, an old friend of yours.

JOHNNY: Louie! (*Enter* LOUIE MEJÍA.)

BERTA: ¿No le reconoces, Johnny? Es Louie Mejía.

JOHNNY: ¡Pinche Louie!

BERTA: ¿Cómo fuiste capaz de matarlo? Why, you were the best of camaradas.

JOHNNY: Yeah, well, cagó el palo. (*Circling* LOUIE. *Drums reach a crescendo.*)

BERTA: You fought because of Ana, ¿verdad?

JOHNNY: Yeah, it all started with that stupid bet to see who would make it with the most rucas in one year. We promised to meet here to compare notes. The winner was to win mil bolas.

LOUIE: (*Embracing and shaking* JOHNNY's *hand.*)   Órale, Johnny, mucho tiempo que no te vidrios. ¡Watcha tu tacuche!

JOHNNY: (*Posing, motioning to his suit.*) That's right, from my brim to my taps—reet pleat.

LOUIE: ¡Puro relajo, carajo!

JOHNNY: Pues, ponte abusado, rajado. (*Motioning to* BERTA.) Berta, dos frías.

LOUIE: Same old Johnny. No has cambiado ni un pito. Hombre, this year went by fast, ¿que no? Órale, let's see who is the badest culero in all of San Anto, Tejas. ¿Tienes tus mil bolas?

JOHNNY: (*Laying it down on the table.*) Simón, un grand, dale gas.

LOUIE: Cuando me largué del high school me fui directamente para México.

JOHNNY: When you crossed the Río Grande, did you do the backstroke?

LOUIE: No, hombre, I drove across the bridge en my Low Rider con mi Zoot Suit. The batos went babas, and the huisas went wild. Me fui hasta el D.F.-tú sabes, la mera capirucha.

JOHNNY: What the hell's a "capirucha?"

LOUIE: It means the CAP, the capital. Dig, México is shaped like a huge pirámide, desde la costa hasta la capital. You should check it out.

JOHNNY: Puro pedo. Nunca fui and I ain't going. My folks worked like dogs para largarse.

LOUIE: Well, you don't know what you're missing, ese. Me metí con una de esas niñas popis, las que viven en Lomas de Chapultepec y van de compras en la Zona Rosa.

JOHNNY: You mean, like, she was a Valley Girl?

LOUIE: For sure. Bueno, I turned on some of that Chicano charm and promised to marry her. Su mami nos cachó cochando, ves. Pero la noche antes de la boda me largué con la hermana menor.

BERTA: (*Who has been eavesdropping with* DON JUAN *as the boys guffaw with laughter.*) ¡Qué desgraciado!

LOUIE: I promised to take her with me to Disneylandia pero, nel pastel. ¡Puras papas! La dejé plantada en Monterrey y me largué para San Antonio.

JOHNNY: 'Ta cabrón, Louie. But only two chicks in one year? (*Signals* BERTA *for a couple of tequilas.*) That's not a very good score.

LOUIE: Once I got back to San Anto me clavé 54 más for a grand total of 56!

JOHNNY: How do I know your count is true?

LOUIE: (*Grabbing* BERTA's *hand as she serves them.*) Nomás párate en cualquier esquina del barrio. Count the babes that pass by with my initials tatooed on their hand. (*BERTA slaps his hand, the boys laugh.*)

JOHNNY: ¡Órale pues!

LOUIE: Top that, chingón!

JOHNNY: I took the Greyhound al norte—to the Big Manzana. New York, New York—so big you gotta say it twice. Ended up in Spanish Harlem. One thing I noticed, if I told people I was a Puerto Rican they treated me like dirt.

LOUIE: ¿No quieren a los puertorriqueños allá?

JOHNNY: Nope, the gringos treat them like "Mescins" in Texas.

LOUIE: ¡Qué gacho!

JOHNNY: But if I told the bolillos I was a Chicano, they were really nice to me.

LOUIE: ¿Por qué?

JOHNNY: I don't know, something to do with "good karma."

LOUIE: Karma? What's karma?

JOHNNY: I don't know, something to do with the Indians. I think it has to do with Mexican food or the pyramids.

LOUIE: No hombre, knowing you, les dijiste que eras "Spanish."

JOHNNY: Hey man, you know I would never deny mi Raza. Anyway, we used to make menudo sometimes and invite the gringos over for breakfast. Of course, we knew they wouldn't eat it if we told them it was pancita de res. So we served it as "American Indian Stew!" they scarfed it up!

LOUIE: ¡Qué loco!

JOHNNY: Pinches gringos. Hey, but the white girls—¡mamasotas! They had never laid—and I do mean LAID—eyes on such a handsome Chicano like me. I ate them up. Anglos, Jews, Czechs, Irish, Italians, Swedes ... it was like the United Nations. I took them away from their fathers, boyfriends, husbands. I would even go down to the Port Authority and pick up runaways. (*Flashback. Flutes and drums. Enter* ANA *in blonde wig dressed as a "RUNAWAY."* JOHNNY *walks into the bus station.*) Hey, Mama, what's happening? Where you from, girl?

RUNAWAY: California.

JOHNNY: Califas? So am I! What part?

RUNAWAY: San Diego.

JOHNNY: San Dedo! All right, I'm from San Diego myself. What a coincidence.

RUNAWAY: Really?

JOHNNY: You're my homegirl. Hey, you wanna go party? I got some marihuana. You look like you're hungry. You wanna go get a hamburger?

RUNAWAY: No thanks.

JOHNNY: (*Giving her money.*) Here, have some bread. You can buy something to eat. Go ahead, take it, man, I'll check you later. (*He walks away.*)

RUNAWAY: Wait a minute ...

JOHNNY: This your first time in the city? (*She nods her head "yes."*) What are you doing here?

RUNAWAY: I ran away from home.

JOHNNY: You ran away from home? (JOHNNY *picks up her bag.*) I got a nice pad you can stay at. How old are you, anyways?

RUNAWAY: Eighteen, Well, fourteen, really. (JOHNNY *takes her by the hand. She exits. End of flashback.*)

BERTA: (*To* DON JUAN.) That's what I forgot, marihuana! (BERTA *takes some marihuana cigarettes and places them on the altar.*)

JOHNNY: Then I turned them out on the streets to turn tricks.

LOUIE: You pimped them?

JOHNNY: Yeah. I was actually doing them a favor. I sprang them out of jail if they got busted, had the doc check them out for social diseases. I took care of my ladies, bro. Besides, some other dude would have got them if I didn't.

LOUIE: ¡Qué desmadre! ¿Y cuántas en total?

JOHNNY: Seventy-two. Six I married. You lose. Pay up!

LOUIE: No te lo creo.

JOHNNY: (*Tossing a packet of legal documents on the table.*) Here's the paternity suits and copies of the police records. I should have been a Turk, I had a fucking harem.

LOUIE: ¡Qué bárbaro! ¡Y puras gringas! (*Looking over the documents.*)

JOHNNY: They're the easiest.

LOUIE: ¿Por qué?

JOHNNY: Women's Lib.

LOUIE:

¿Cuántas horas has de emplear
Para cada ruca que vas a amar?

JOHNNY: One hour to fall in love with them. Another to make it with them. A third to abandon them and sixty seconds to forget them.

LOUIE: ¡Chingao! No puedo compararme contigo. (*Giving* JOHNNY *his money.*)

JOHNNY: Why try? There's only one Johnny Tenorio! (*Scooping up the money.*)

LOUIE: Alguien te lo va a cobrar un día.

JOHNNY: Tan largo me lo fías. (BERTA, DON JUAN *and* LOUIE *do a double take on that line.*) But say, would you like a chance to win your money back?

LOUIE: ¡Simón que yes!

JOHNNY: You have a sister.

LOUIE: Ana?

JOHNNY: She's fine.

LOUIE: Estás loco, apenas tiene quince años.

JOHNNY: I told you I like fresh meat.

LOUIE: ¡Ahora sí que me estás cayendo gordo, buey!

JOHNNY: ¿A ver? ¿No crees que la puedo hacer caer?

LOUIE: Ponte abusado, ¡malvado!

JOHNNY: ¡No me chingues, chango!

LOUIE: ¡Puro pedo, puto! (*They go for each other, knocking down chairs, glasses, etc. They both pull out knives at the same time.* JOHNNY *disarms* LOUIE, *knocks him down and is about to stab him when* BERTA *stops him with a wave of her hand.*)

BERTA: ¡Cálmala, Johnny! (LOUIE *freezes.*)

JOHNNY: What?

BERTA: Ya lo mataste una vez. Do you want to kill him again?

JOHNNY: (*Backing off.*) Pues no, not if he's already dead.

BERTA: ¡Qué lástima, Johnny!—you had a lot of good times together.

JOHNNY: Yeah.

BERTA: Era como tu hermano, you married his sister. ¿Por qué lo hiciste? (LOUIE *exits.*)

JOHNNY: No sé, Berta, it was either him or me. La Ley del Barrio. (JOHNNY *exits.*)

DON JUAN: ¡Ya no puede ver más! (*Taking off his mask.*)

BERTA: ¿Cómo que no?

DON JUAN: ¡Qué triste tragedia!

BERTA: Más parece una comedia. Ándale—sit back, have another tequila. (*Going to pour him another shot.*)

DON JUAN: (*Stopping her hand.*) ¡No quiero más!

BERTA: At least you know when to stop—él no.

DON JUAN: Do you think that the sins of the father are visited upon the son?

BERTA: Don Juan, con todo respeto, I am not here to accuse anyone. I am merely telling Johnny's story, an old cuento todos conocen. Algunos dicen que empezó en España, others say it is a legacy of the Moors. All I know is él vive—in all of us.

DON JUAN: Síguele pues. (*Putting his mask back on.*)

BERTA: Ahora llamaré al espíritu de Ana. (*Flutes and drums. Enter* ANA *in a Catholic schoolgirl uniform, carrying her schoolbooks.*) Ana, as she once was. Johnny! Johnny! Tell us what happened to Ana. Don't tell me you didn't love her. Yo te conozco, mosco.

JOHNNY: (*Re-entering.*) Love? I don't know what the word means, Berta.

BERTA: Why didn't you try to learn more about el verdadero amor, Johnny, rather than playing at it.

JOHNNY: I'm a player, Berta.

BERTA: Then, play this scene out. (BERTA *snaps her fingers.*)

JOHNNY: (*Crossing to* ANA.) Hi, Ana!

ANA: Hello Johnny. Are you looking for Louie?

JOHNNY: No, I was looking for you.

ANA: Me?

JOHNNY: Can I give you a ride somewhere?

ANA: No thanks, I have to get to school.

JOHNNY: I've been wanting to talk to you.

ANA: Really? About what?

JOHNNY: Things weighing heavy on my mind. (ANA *stops,* JOHNNY *touches her shoulder.*) Your skin is so soft and fine.

ANA: Excuse me, but I'm late for class.

JOHNNY: Do you want to go cruising after school?

ANA: I don't know. I have a lot of homework. I really have to go now. Bye! (ANA *turns away from* JOHNNY, *freezes.*)

BERTA: So, you weren't very successful at first, eh?

JOHNNY: No. But I never gave up. I waited for her every day after school. You see, that's how you break down their resistance.

BERTA: Hmmmm. Cuéntame.

JOHNNY: Well, one day we had a coke at the Cinco y Diez. (ANA *unfreezes as they both sit down at a table.*) So, there, you see? I'm not going to bite.

ANA: You have such a reputation as a lady-killer. They say you're after one thing and one thing only.

JOHNNY: Sure, I can get plenty of girls. Every day, every hour, every minute if I want to. But there's more to it than that.

ANA: What do you look for in a girl?

JOHNNY: Someone I can talk to. Sometimes I wish I had a sister just like you.

ANA: Don't you have any women friends? You know, just friends.

JOHNNY: Sure, one of my best friends is Berta, the bartender at Big Berta's Bar on Guadalupe Street.

ANA: What's she like?

JOHNNY: She's someone I can tell my troubles to. She listens to me and makes the pain go away.

ANA: I'll listen to you, Johnny.

JOHNNY: (*Rising up to leave.*) Well, listen, it is kind of crowded here. Wouldn't you rather go to my place? (ANA *freezes.*)

BERTA: (*Butting in.*) Just a minute here. You really think you know a lot about us mujeres, don't you?

JOHNNY: Yeah, well, that's what I studied in school, Berta.

BERTA: What school? You dropped out.

JOHNNY: The School of Love, baby. That's how come I knew Ana was grade "A." It took me three months of lecturing before she took her final exam. Sabes qué, Berta, maybe it's true what they say about us Latin Lovers.

BERTA: Johnny, esa cosa de los Latin Lovers es un myth.

JOHNNY: Exactly!

BERTA: Bueno pues, entonces—¿qué pasó?

JOHNNY: Hey, the serpent got Eva to eat the apple, ¿que no? (*Crossing to* ANA)

ANA: So, this is your famous apartment.

JOHNNY: What, you don't like it?

ANA: No, it's just I've heard so much about it, I can't believe I'm here.

JOHNNY: Well, from now on you're going to be the only one.

ANA: Ay, Johnny, you're just saying that.

JOHNNY: No, I'm not. See this? (*Matching his palms to hers.*) A gypsy told me how to find the right match. (*Romantic guitar music plays.*)

ANA: Your hand is bigger than mine.

JOHNNY: Ah, but our love lines match!

ANA: Do you believe in all that? Do you really think you'll ever find a woman that'll really satisfy you?

JOHNNY: (*Kissing her.*) I think I just did. (*He holds her close.*)

ANA: Johnny ... don't.

JOHNNY: Why not?

ANA: I want it to be special. (JOHNNY *opens her blouse.*)

JOHNNY: You are special to me, Ann, really. (JOHNNY *goes down on his knees.*) I adore you, I worship you! (*Lights begin to fade on them.*)

BERTA: (*To* DON JUAN.) Does this look familiar, Don Juan?

DON JUAN: Desgraciadamente.

BERTA: (*Calling out.*) Bueno, Johnny, dime, did Ana change you?

JOHNNY: She did, Berta, she did. You might say she deflected me from the meteorite course of my destiny.

BERTA: Where did you learn such big words, Johnny?

JOHNNY: I didn't go to college, but I'm not stupid. I even know a little Shaky-es-pear!

BERTA: Bueno pues, sigue el cuento.

ANA: (*Entering, buttoning her blouse.*) Well, its over. You got what you wanted, right?

JOHNNY: I want more than that, Ann.

ANA: Like what?

JOHNNY: Your alma.

ANA: (*Turning to go.*) Adiós.

JOHNNY: Come on, baby, you're not mad at me, are you?

ANA: I guess I'm just mad at myself.

JOHNNY: Where are you going?

ANA: Home. It's late. Mis padres are probably wondering what happened to me.

JOHNNY: Stay here. You don't have to go home. You're a woman now, mi mujer.

ANA: I don't think so, bato. And stop calling me "Ann." Mi nombre es Ana.

JOHNNY: ¡Ana, pues! Ana, you've touched me somewhere I didn't know existed, here en mi corazón. When you're not around me duele.

ANA: Even if it was true, it's just not going to work. I'm only fifteen and you're twenty. Mi hermano will kill you.

JOHNNY: Ana, do you know the story of Romeo and Juliet?

ANA: Of course, I saw the movie.

JOHNNY: Well, Juliet was only fourteen, and she had a relative who hated Romeo. Yet, their amor survived for all time.

ANA: But they both died, cabrón! No thanks! I like you, Johnny, te quiero mucho. But you're nothing but trouble for a girl. I don't know why I went to bed with you in the first place, por pendeja.

JOHNNY: Because you wanted to, Ana. It's our destino. Look, I used to run around with las gringas. They wanted to get

down, tú sabes, get married and have kids. But I couldn't.
I was searching, sin saberlo, for a Chicana.

ANA: Oh, Johnny.

JOHNNY: Someone of my own Raza ...

ANA: Stop it ...

JOHNNY: Como tú.

ANA: I want to believe you sooooo much.

JOHNNY: Ana, I'd do anything for you.

ANA: Anything?

JOHNNY: Sí.

ANA: Then, wait for me.

JOHNNY: Wait for you?

ANA: If you love me you'll wait until I finish high school. You'll
wait for me like a real amigo.

JOHNNY: ¡Amigo! You mean you don't want to fuck me!

ANA: See! I knew it! That's the only thing you want. ¡Te odio!

JOHNNY: Bueno, bueno. We'll do it your way.

ANA: No te lo creo, not one word!

JOHNNY: (*Embracing her.*) I'll prove it to you, mi amor. Just
give me a chance. Lo haré por ti. (*Kissing her.*)

ANA: ¿De veras, Johnny? You promise? (JOHNNY *nods his head
"yes." A long passionate kiss.* ANA *backs away into another "space."*)

BERTA: How long did you remain "friends," Johnny?

JOHNNY: Long enough, long enough.

ANA: (*On another part of the stage,* ANA *has run into* LOUIE.)
You're not going to tell me who to see and who not to see.

LOUIE: Anybody but him, Ana, él es veneno.

ANA: Es mi amigo, my best friend.

LOUIE: ¡Es un hijo de la chingada!

ANA: Don't talk that way about him.

LOUIE: Sólo estoy tratando de cuidarte. I know him very well.

ANA: Like you know yourself, Mr. Hipócrita? The word was out
on you, big brother—find 'em, fuck 'em and forget 'em.

LOUIE: Okay. Eso era antes. You know I'm getting married to
Inés. Sure, I used to do that stuff, but you have to grow
up sometime. Johnny nunca va a ser hombre.

ANA: If you can do it, why not Johnny? Louie, we're all very
proud of you, going to night school, working days. And
now you're getting married to a wonderful girl. But you
have to let me live my own life. I'm sixteen years old now,
no soy una esquincle.

LOUIE: But you don't understand this guy—créelo cuando te digo, he's a worm, a víbora, a vampire. He'll suck your blood and leave you dry! Si lo veo contigo, lo mato, I'll kill him! (*Exit* LOUIE.)

ANA: (*Going over to* JOHNNY *and hugging him.*) I don't care what anybody says about you; te quiero, I love you with all my corazón.

JOHNNY: I won't disappoint you, Ana. What you've told me has changed my way of thinking. I'm going to talk to your padres and ask for your hand in marriage.

ANA: Yeah, but I have to finish school, find a career.

JOHNNY: Don't worry, I'll put you through college! And I'm going to clean up my act, no more hustling or selling drugs. I'm going to get a regular job.

ANA: Johnny, I know you can do it.

JOHNNY: Yeah, it's time I stopped acting like a punk kid and started acting como un hombre.

ANA: (*Pulling out a cross and chain.*) Johnny, here, it's a cross the monjas gave me for my First Holy Communion.

JOHNNY: No, I couldn't, really.

ANA: Please, I want you to have it. When you're in trouble think about me. It will give you strength.

JOHNNY: (*Taking the cross, reluctantly.*) Yes, I'm going to need lots of prayers.

ANA: What do you mean?

JOHNNY: Well, before I start my new life, you see, I'm going to have to pay off all my debts. I owe some very important gente a lot of lana.

ANA: Well, they're just going to have to wait.

JOHNNY: You don't understand, Ana. These people don't wait for anybody. They want their money now, or they break your legs.

ANA: Don't worry, Johnny, we'll find a way. Mi cruz nunca falla, my cross never fails. (ANA *exits.* JOHNNY *walks towards the bar, sadly fingering the cross.*)

BERTA: That was two years ago. ¿Nunca terminó Ana la high school?

JOHNNY: No, she had to go out and get a job.

BERTA: ¿Y qué de la universidad y su career?

JOHNNY: Why are you asking me these questions, Berta?

BERTA: La dejaste embarazada, didn't you?

JOHNNY: Pregnant—yes! That's what she wanted!

BERTA: Off course, nunca te casaste con ella. (BERTA *takes the cross away from* JOHNNY *and places it reverently on the altar.*)

JOHNNY: No, but we were living together, isn't that the same damn thing!

DON JUAN: (*Suddenly exploding in a fit of anger.*) No puedo escucharte, vil Johnny, porque recelo que hay algún rayo en el cielo preparado a aniquilarte.

JOHNNY: What's that you say, viejo?

DON JUAN: Ah! No pudiendo creer lo que de ti me decían, confiando en que mentían, vine esta noche a verte. Sigue, pues, con ciego afán en tu torpe frenesí; más nunca vuelvas a mí. No te conozco, Johnny.

JOHNNY: (*Advancing towards him.*) What the hell do I care what you think.

DON JUAN: Adiós, pues. Mas, no te olvides de que hay un Dios justiciero.

JOHNNY: (*Grabbing* DON JUAN.) Just a Goddamn minute!

DON JUAN: ¿Qué quieres?

JOHNNY: Who are you? Take off that mask.

DON JUAN: (*Pushing him off.*) No, en vano me lo pides.

JOHNNY: (*Unmasking him.*) Show me your face!

DON JUAN: ¡Villano!

JOHNNY: ¡Papá!

BERTA: That's right, Johnny, es tu padre. You haven't seen him in años, ever since you left home to raise hell. (*Flutes and drums. Slow motion flashback.* JOHNNY *reverts to age seven.* DON JUAN *becomes a much younger man.*) What was it like when you were chico, Johnny? ¿No lo quisiste?

JOHNNY: Papá, no quiero ir a la escuela.

DON JUAN: Pero hijo, tienes que ir.

JOHNNY: Papá, todos los bolillos hacen fun de mí.

DON JUAN: Cómo que hacen "fun" de ti?

JOHNNY: Durante el lonche, todos ellos comen sanwiches. Cuando saco mis tacos, se empiezan a reír.

DON JUAN: No les hagas caso.

JOHNNY: Y un día mi paper bag estaba greasy y me llamaron "greaser."

DON JUAN: Okay. Empezando mañana puedes llevar sanwiches.

JOHNNY: Okay. ¡Qué suave! (*Thinking about it.*) Sabes qué, mejor no. No me gustan los sanwiches de frijol ... ni de chorizo.

DON JUAN: Bueno, ya apúrate, que se está haciendo tarde.

JOHNNY: No quiero ir, Papá, hacen fun de mí—especialmente la "tee-cher."

DON JUAN: La "tee-shirt?" ¿La camiseta?

JOHNNY: No, la tee-shirt no, la "tee-cher," Mrs. Blaha.

DON JUAN: (*Laughing.*) ¡Oh, la maestra, la Señora Blaha! ¿Qué dice ella?

JOHNNY: After playground me dijo, "Johnny, washe you hans porque dey durty." Me las lavé y entonces me hizo show them en front of everybody.

DON JUAN: ¿Y qué?

JOHNNY: Entonces dijo, "Well, Johnny, you hans so braun I can tell if they clean o no!"

DON JUAN: Ahora sí que no ...

JOHNNY: Y un día la tee-cher me llamó un bad nombre—me llamó "spic."

DON JUAN: ¡No me digas! ¡Conque te llamó "spic!"

JOHNNY: Sí, dijo, "Johnny, you no no how to spick good English!"

DON JUAN: ¡Ay, mi hijo! Por eso tienes que ir a la escuela. Tu mamacita y yo, que en paz descanse, no pudimos ir. ¿No ves como tienes problemas con el Inglich?

JOHNNY: A mí no me importa. ¡No quiero hablar el English!

DON JUAN: ¡No, eso no! ¡Me lo vas a aprender a huevo! Mira nomás. Estoy trabajando como un burro para que puedas educarte.

JOHNNY: I don't care. Trabajo como un burro yo también!

DON JUAN: No, señor. Un hijo mío nunca se raja.

JOHNNY: Pero el Gregy Weiner me quiere beat up. Mira, he hit me right here. (*Enter* LOUIE *in a blonde wig, dressed as* "GREGY.") Can I play with you?

GREGY: No, you can't even speak English, beaner.

JOHNNY: Don't you call me dat!

GREGY: What are you going to do about it, beaner! Brown like a bean! Chili dipper!

JOHNNY: No, I'm not!

GREGY: Yes, you are! (*Hitting* JOHNNY.)

DON JUAN: (*As* JOHNNY *cries.*) ¡Te pegó y no se lo regresaste! ¡Ve y dale en la madre!

JOHNNY: Pero, he's bigger than me!

DON JUAN: Ya te dije, un hijo mío no se raja. ¡Pégale! Si no, yo te pego a ti.

GREGY: Spic! Greaser! Wetback!

JOHNNY: (*Rushing in, flailing with his fists, he gets a lucky shot on* GREGY.) Gringo! Gabacho! Redneck!

GREGY: Teacher! Teacher! (*Running off.*)

DON JUAN: ¡Ahora sí eres hombre! ¿Por qué lloras? Solo las mujeres y los jotos lloran. Ni modo, Johnny, tuviste que aprender a huevo. Ahora, dime, ¿qué dijiste que querías ser cuando seas grande?

JOHNNY: Un astronaut, Papá.

DON JUAN: Ya ves, el primer astronauta chicano. Por eso tienes que ir a la escuela. Vas a ser el primer astronauta que come tacos en el espacio. ·

JOHNNY: Wow! Tacos in outer space!

DON JUAN: ¡Y mira lo que tengo para mi astronauta! (*Giving* JOHNNY *a new lunch pail.*)

JOHNNY: Oh boy, Papá, un Star Wars lunch pail! (DON JUAN *starts walking away from* JOHNNY. *End of flashback.*) ¿Papá? ¡Papá! Pa ... pá.

DON JUAN: (*As the older man.*) ¡Mientes, no lo fui jamás!

JOHNNY: Then ... go to hell!

DON JUAN: ¡Hijos como tú son hijos de Satanás!

JOHNNY: Fuck you!

DON JUAN: Johnny, en brazos del vicio desolado te abandono. Me matas, mas te perdono. Que Dios es el Santo Juicio. (DON JUAN *exits.*)

BERTA: (JOHNNY *drops down on his knees and bows his head, clutching his lunchpail.* BERTA *goes and tries to console him.*) Triqui tran, triqui tran; los maderos de San Juan. (*Singing a haunting melody as she runs her fingers through his hair.*) Piden pan, no les dan; piden queso, les dan un hueso que se les atoran en el pescuezo. (*Beat.*) Did you love your papá, Johnny?

JOHNNY: Yeah, I guess so. But, that's life in the big city.

BERTA: Do you know that you and your father are very much alike? (BERTA *takes the lunch pail and places it reverently on the altar.*)

JOHNNY: What are you doing?

BERTA: Nada, Johnny, just picking up the pieces.

JOHNNY: You're playing some kind of weird game here, aren't you, Berta?

BERTA: No es un juego, it's for real.

JOHNNY: Why did you bring my father into this?

BERTA: Tu padre te crió—he raised you after your mother died, ¿verdad?

JOHNNY: I didn't need him, I didn't need nobody.

BERTA: Nunca lo conociste, just like you never knew your mother.

JOHNNY: You know my mother died when I was born.

BERTA: Era una mujer muy hermosa.

JOHNNY: That's probably where I get my good looks.

BERTA: Sabes qué, she looked a lot like Ana. (*Flutes and drums, enter* ANA, *pregnant, as* JOHNNY's MOTHER.)

JOHNNY: Mamá ...

BERTA: She was pregnant with you. Tu papá había recién llegado de la Ciudad de México con su sobrina, María. (*Enter* DON JUAN *as a young man.*)

MOTHER: Is your niece all settled in the spare bedroom?

DON JUAN: Sí, no te preocupes por ella. En México vivía amontonada en un cuarto con tres hermanas.

MOTHER: She's a very pretty girl.

DON JUAN: Sí, alguien se la va a robar uno de estos días. ¿Cómo te sientes, querida?

MOTHER: I think the baby is going to be a varón—he kicks like a little bull.

DON JUAN: Un torito. Lo nombraremos Juan, como yo, como mi padre.

MOTHER: Johnny!

DON JUAN: ¡Juan, mi hijo no va a ser gringo! Ojalá que salga como mi padre, alto y güero con ojos verdes. Todas las mujeres estaban locas por él.

MOTHER: Wasn't your mother jealous?

DON JUAN: ¿Qué podía decir? Los hombres—hombres, el trigo—trigo.

MOTHER: ¡Ay sí!

DON JUAN: Tuvo tres mujeres, aparte de mi madre. ¡Tengo hermanos por dondequiera!

MOTHER: How horrible!

DON JUAN: Pero nunca se casó con otra. Oh no, mi madre era su único amor.

MOTHER: I don't want to name our son after a mujeriego.

DON JUAN: Mujer, mis padres duraron casados cincuenta años.

MOTHER: Juan, that doesn't mean tu madre didn't suffer.

DON JUAN: Mamá adoraba a mi padre, tanto como él la adoraba.

MOTHER: What if it's a niña, what will we name her then?

DON JUAN: ¡Juana!

MOTHER: Nooo. Let's name her after a flower, como Rosa, Iris o Azalea.

DON JUAN: No, no, no. Las flores se recogen facilitas. Mejor
    Rosario, Guadalupe, Concepción. O María, como mi so-
    brina.
MOTHER: Why?
DON JUAN: Porque una hembra deber ser santa o ángel.
MOTHER: ¡Ay, sí! (*Beat.*) As if your niece was so saintly!
DON JUAN: ¿Por qué dices eso, mujer?
MOTHER: Men shouldn't expect us to act the Virgen María while
    they go out and do what they please.
DON JUAN: Esas ideas te las metieron los gringos. Eso es lo que
    no me gusta de este país.
MOTHER: What, that we're more liberated than in the old coun-
    try? Mira, Juan, what would you do if you caught your
    daughter sleeping around?
DON JUAN: Como dicen los pochos, I'll break her neck!
MOTHER: See how you men are!
DJ & JOHNNY: (*At the same time.* DON JUAN *to the* MOTHER,
    JOHNNY *to* BERTA.) Why are you telling me this?
BERTA: Para que aprendas, Johnny. (*With a wave of her hands,*
    BERTA *changes the tone of the scene.*) Look what hap-
    pened a few days later ...
MOTHER: (*Angry now.*) What were you doing in María's room?
DON JUAN: Nada, querida, nomás quería saber si estaba bien.
MOTHER: (*Seemingly directing her comments to* JOHNNY.) ¡Men-
    tiroso! Now I know where you go at night!
JOHNNY: (*Responding to* MOTHER.) No, no ...
DON JUAN: ¡Te lo juro por Diosito Santo!
MOTHER: (*Back and forth, to both men.*) Tu sobrina, your own
    niece! How could you!
DON JUAN: No es mi sobrina.
JOHNNY: Then what was she?
BERTA: María was your father's amante, his lover.
MOTHER: (*Falling, clutching her stomach.*) ¡Ay, Dios mío!
BERTA: On top of that, he married her in Mexico.
DON JUAN: Mi amor, querida, ¿qué pasa?
JOHNNY: (*To* DON JUAN.) Don't just stand there, get a doctor.
    (*Exit* DON JUAN. JOHNNY *goes to* MOTHER.) ¡Mamá!
    ¡Mamacita! Please don't die!
MOTHER: Promise you'll never betray me!
JOHNNY: I swear, I swear! Juro por Dios Santo.
BERTA: (MOTHER *dies.*) She died shortly after giving birth to
    you.
JOHNNY: ¡Mamá!

BERTA: Of a broken heart.

JOHNNY: ¿Por qué lo hizo? Why did he do it?

BERTA: Your father paid for it, Johnny. Juan cesó de ser Don Juan. That's why he never remarried.

JOHNNY: Why didn't he tell me?

BERTA: He didn't want you to be like him.

JOHNNY: Oh, my God. I see it all now.

BERTA: What, Johnny?

JOHNNY: The curse!

BERTA: ¿La maldición?

JOHNNY: I'm damned for all time!

BERTA: Do I detect repentance in your voice?

JOHNNY: (*Screaming.*) Hell no!

BERTA: ¿No? (BERTA *starts lighting the candles on the altar. Incense burns.*) Quizás entonces tu deseo se hará realidad.

JOHNNY: What wish?

BERTA: Your death wish.

JOHNNY: What are you talking about?

BERTA: Life after death, la inmortalidad. I lit these velas to show you a vision. See how brightly they burn? Smell the copal incense, the kind the ancients used in their sacred rites. Pray, Johnny, ruega a la Virgen de Guadalupe, Nuestra Señora, Tonantzín.

JOHNNY: ¡Mis ojos!

BERTA: Pronto vas a ver. Now we wait for the souls to return. They'll come to say a few final words.

JOHNNY: I don't want to hear it, Berta. No one ever really cared about me, not my father, not Ana, none of them.

BERTA: (*Serving him food and drink.*) Cálmate. Sit. Mira, I fixed your favorite comida—tamales y atole. Eat. Los otros están por llegar.

JOHNNY: All right. That's more like it. Be sure to invite Louie. Except that he has so many holes in his stomach, I doubt that the food will stay in.

BERTA: No debes burlarte de los muertos, Johnny.

JOHNNY: Hey, Louie! I'm calling you out, man! Berta made some ricos tamales and hot atole. Better hurry before I eat it all up! (LOUIE, *wearing a calavera mask, enters.*)

BERTA: (*Noticing* LOUIE.) Ah, Louie, there you are. Te traigo un plato. You boys have such big appetites, hay que calentar más tamales. (BERTA *exits.*)

JOHNNY: (*Still absorbed in his food.*) Yeah, Louie, sit down and
    ... (*Suddenly noticing him.*) Oh! Another appearance,
    eh? What's with the costume, still playing trick or treat?

LOUIE: ¡Te dije que no te acercaras a Ana!

JOHNNY: (*Pulling out a gun.*) Chíngate, cabrón, nobody tells
    me what to do! (LOUIE *lunges for* JOHNNY, *who shoots*
    LOUIE *in the head.*) I told you not to mess with me!
    (LOUIE *does not fall—he keeps advancing.*) Jesus Christ!

LOUIE: Remember, I'm already dead! ¿Qué te pasa, Johnny?
    ¿Tienes miedo? ¡Tú, el mero chingón! (*Grabbing*
    JOHNNY *by the throat.*)

JOHNNY: ¡Ayyyyyy! ¡Déjame! Let me go!

LOUIE: (*Dragging* JOHNNY *over to the table.*) No me digas que
    sientes la presencia de la Muerte!

JOHNNY: Get away from me!

LOUIE: (*Grabbing* JOHNNY *by his hair.*) Come! Come! Que ésta
    va a ser tu última cena. (*Pushing his face into the plate,*
    forcing him to eat.)

JOHNNY: What is this horrible stuff?

LOUIE: Tamales de ceniza. (*Forcing him to drink.*)

JOHNNY: Ashes!

LOUIE: ¡Atole de fuego!

JOHNNY: Fire! Why do you make me eat this?

LOUIE: Te doy lo que tú serás.

JOHNNY: Fire and ashes!

LOUIE: ¡Morderás el polvo!

JOHNNY: No!

BERTA: Ya se va terminando tu existencia y es tiempo de pronun-
    ciar tu sentencia.

JOHNNY: My time is not up!

LOUIE: Faltan cinco para las doce. A la media noche no se te
    conoce. Y aquí que vienen conmigo, los que tu eterno
    castigo de Dios reclamando están. (*Enter* ANA *and* DON
    JUAN, *also calaveras. They block* JOHNNY's *escape.*)

JOHNNY: Ann!

ANA: Yes, it's me.

JOHNNY: ¡Papá!

DON JUAN: Si, mi hijo.

JOHNNY: (*Tries to jump behind the bar. Enter* BERTA *dressed as*
    La Catrina with skull mask.) Berta!

BERTA: No hay escape, Johnny. You must face them.

JOHNNY: You too!

BERTA: No estoy aquí para juzgarte, Johnny—they are.

DON JUAN: Un punto de contrición da a un alma la salvación y ese punto aún te lo dan.

LOUIE: ¡Imposible! ¿En un momento borrar veinte años malditos de crimenes y delitos?

JOHNNY: Berta! Will I really be saved if I repent?

BERTA: Yes, but only if one of your victims forgives you on this the Day of the Dead.

JOHNNY: (*In a heavily accented Spanish.*) Entonces, perdónenme ustedes, yo no quiero morir. Deseo pedirles disculpas a todos los que hice sufrir.

LOUIE: Empezaremos conmigo, que soy el más ofendido. ¿Por qué me acuchillaste? ¿Por qué te me echaste encima?

JOHNNY: There's no excuse. But it was a fair fight among men. You wanted to be like me, Louie, but you lost, and that's the price you had to pay.

LOUIE: ¿Ven? No tiene excusa. Que lo aparezca la lechuza. Si de mi piel hizo carnicera, ¡él también será calavera! (*The feeling of this last scene is that of a bullfight. JOHNNY is the bull and the others are wielding the cape, pike and banderillas.*)

BERTA: ¿Quién sigue?

ANA: (*She is dressed like a whore.*) I am next.

JOHNNY: Ana. You don't want to see me dead, think of our children.

ANA: I am thinking of them. I would rather they not know you, for fear they will become like you.

JOHNNY: No, no, no! I swear to God—I'll change!

BERTA: You repent?

JOHNNY: Sí, I promise to go home and be a good padre y esposo.

ANA: ¡Mentiras! I've heard all this before. He'll go back to chasing women and drinking first change he gets.

JOHNNY: Ana, don't you see I have to change, my life depends on it.

ANA: No, Johnny, you're addicted to your vicios. You contaminate everyone. Look, I gave you all my love and you turned me out to turn tricks!

JOHNNY: But the Mafiosos were going to kill me. You agreed to do it. I didn't force you!

ANA: You manipulated me, Johnny, like you did all the others.

JOHNNY: But Ana, don't you see, it's a curse that's been passed down from generation to generation. I'm a victim, you're a victim, ¡todos somos víctimas!

ANA: That's right, blame everybody but yourself!

JOHNNY: Ana, honey, think about it. You tried to control me, you wanted to channel my energy.

ANA: I wanted a family!

JOHNNY: But I'm not an esposo. I am a hunter!

ANA: (*Laying into him with a vengeance.*) Si mi corazón murió en esa carrera, ¡el mujeriego también será calavera! (*A mournful cry escapes* JOHNNY*'s lips.*)

BERTA: ¿Alguien más? Time is almost up.

JOHNNY: ¡Papá! How can you stand there and say nothing after what you did!

DON JUAN: Ya lo sé, y me arrepentiré hasta mis últimos días. Después que murió tu madre, traté de encaminarte hacia una vida mejor. Fracasé. Seguiste la vía chueca.

JOHNNY: Hypocrite!

DON JUAN: Johnny, dile a Dios que te perdone, como Él me perdonó.

JOHNNY: You want me to ask God for a pardon?

DON JUAN: Es lo único que tienes que hacer.

BERTA: Go on, Johnny, ask for forgiveness.

JOHNNY: But I don't believe in God!

DON JUAN: Entonces estás perdido. (JOHNNY *sinks to his knees. Bells toll softly in the distance.*)

BERTA: Johnny, Johnny, you don't really understand what's happening, do you?

JOHNNY: Berta, will you forgive me? (*Throwing himself at her feet, groveling, as though wanting to get back into her womb.*)

BERTA: Johnny, tú nunca me has ofendido.

JOHNNY: I trusted you, Berta. I told you everything.

BERTA: That's right, mi'jo. I cleansed you by listening and understanding. You see, I am the eater of sins, la que se traga los pecados.

JOHNNY: Oh, Berta, you're the only woman I've ever loved! (*Turning to the other skeletons, who have remained deathly still in a silent tableau.*) You see, somebody loves me! (*To* BERTA.) Does this mean I'm saved? Does this mean I've cheated death?

BERTA: No, Johnny. No te burlaste de la muerte. You are already dead.

JOHNNY: What are you talking about!

BERTA: The gringo who caught you in bed with his wife ...

JOHNNY: I killed him!

BERTA: Yes, but he mortally wounded you. Has estado muerto por mucho tiempo.

JOHNNY: But ... how?

BERTA: Tu espíritu, tan violento, no descansaba. Y como este es el Día de los Muertos, the night the souls come back to visit, you returned to your old haunts.

JOHNNY: But, touch me, feel me, I'm alive!

BERTA: Vives solamente en nuestras memorias, Johnny. Te estamos recordando in a celebration ... of death.

JOHNNY: (*Beginning to realize.*) Ohhh noooo!

BERTA: Escucha. ¿Oyes las campanas, Johnny? (*Bells toll.*) Do you hear the women praying rosarios? (*Women praying rosaries.*) See the men digging a grave? (*Pointing offstage.*) Es tu tumba, Johnny.

JOHNNY: I've been dead all this time?

BERTA: Así es, Johnny, todos estamos muertos.

JOHNNY: How can that be?

BERTA: Hay más de una manera de morir. You stabbed Louie to death, but you broke Ana's heart.

JOHNNY: What about my father?

BERTA: His faith in you died.

JOHNNY: Y tú, Berta?

BERTA: Ahhhhh, I am not of the dead, but I am neither of the living. You see, I am of the here, then and will be. Ven, Johnny. (*Flutes and drums. Leading him over to the altar which is suddenly brightly lit.*) Look! This is your altar! (BERTA *climbs up a step. In this light it resembles an Aztec pyramid.*) Look! (*Holding up a calavera mask.*) Aquí está tu máscara ... (*Placing death mask on* JOHNNY's *face.*)

JOHNNY: Am I one of you now! Am I one of the living dead!

BERTA: (*A conch shell blows several times.*) Prepare, Johnny prepárate para la inmortalidad!

JOHNNY: I aaaammmmmm deaaaaaddd!! (JOHNNY *screams, his arms raised up to heaven.*)

BERTA: Here is Johnny Tenorio, el Don Juan, a thorn in the soul of la Raza since time immemorial. Ha traicionado a mujeres, asesinado a hombres y causado gran dolor. Por eso decimos ... que muera!

CHORUS: ¡Que muera!

BERTA: But he also stood alone, defied all the rules, and fought the best he knew how. His heart pounds fiercely inside all of us—the men who desire to be like him, the women

who lust after him. He is our lover, brother, father and
son. Por eso decimos—¡que viva!

CHORUS: ¡Que viva!

JOHNNY: (*After several beats* JOHNNY *jumps down from the altar.*) Pues, entonces, liven up, let's party! (*The other skeletons are scandalized.*) Come on, get the house a round, it's on me! We got all night! (*Grabbing* ANA *and dancing with her.*)

BERTA: Just wait until morning!

The CALAVERAS *grab partners and dance amidst "ajúas" and gritos.*

CORRIDO

Creció la milpa con la lluvia en el potrero
y las palomas van volando al pedregal
bonitos toros llevan hoy al matadero,
que buen caballo va montando el caporal.
Ya las campanas de San Juan están doblando,
todos los fieles se dirigen a rezar,
y por el cerro los rancheros van bajando,
a un hombre muerto que lo llevan a enterrar.
En una choza muy humilde llora un niño,
y las mujeres se aconsejan y se van,
sólo su madre lo consuela con cariño,
mirando al cielo llora y reza por su Juan.
Aquí termino de cantar este corrido
de Juan ranchero, charrasqueado y burlador,
que se creyó de las mujeres consentido,
y fue borracho, parrandero y jugador.

Slow fade as CORRIDO *ends.*

EL FIN

The Savior

CHARACTERS

ARCHBISHOP OSCAR ROMERO
SISTER CELESTINA
FATHER RUTILIO GRANDE (also AMERICAN AMBAS-
SADOR)
FATHER RENÉ REVELO (also BISHOP #3)
FATHER NETO BARRERA (also MAJOR D'ABUSSION,
DEATH SQUAD CALAVERA)
CALAVERA BISHOP ÁLVAREZ (also PAPAL NUNCIO,
TEMPTER)
CALAVERA OLIGARCHY (also BISHOP #2)
CALAVERA PRESIDENTE (also CALAVERA SOLDADO,
BISHOP #1)
CALAVERA CAMPESINA (also AMERICAN REPORTER,
VOICE, CHOIR, SINGER)
also CALAVERAS, CAMPESINOS, SOLDIERS and REBELS

CASTING NOTE

Any number of combinations are possible. The play can be
done with six men and three women.

DESIGN NOTE

"Calaveras" are skulls, by extension, skeletons, in Spanish.
The calavera motif is a Meso-American symbol dating back to pre-
Columbian times. In addition, the story takes place during a civil
war, a war among brothers, where all are killing each other. Other
characters are literally, the "walking dead," because they are dying
of hunger or because of their mind-set. Some are in a stage of
spiritual corruption. Archetypical characters can be more calavera-
like then those who are realistically drawn. This style also allows
one character to wear many different hats.

ACT ONE

At center is the altar where OSCAR ARNULFO ROMERO
*is to be entombed. Up above is a wooden cross on which hangs
an emaciated Christ. Slightly below is a pulpit where* ROMERO
*preaches. At right is some scaffolding indicating repair work and
exposing the wooden ribs of the edifice. Upstage is a stained glass
window on which appear all the projections of scene titles, biblical
quotations and other commentary. The celebrants of this ceremony
sit in the wooden pews and the space between them and the altar is
used as a playing area. The play begins with* ROMERO *dressed in
a bloodstained vestment and alb, speaking to the voice of* SISTER
CELESTINA.

*PALM SUNDAY, MARCH 30, 1980. THE MAIN CATHE-
DRAL. SAN SALVADOR, CENTRAL AMERICA.*

ROMERO: What happened?

CELESTINA: (*Voice off.*) They shot you.

ROMERO: (*Shaking his head. In the light we see that this is the
        face of a dead man.*) Who? What are you talking about?

CELESTINA: You were shot on the altar of the chapel of the Divine
        Providence as you said mass ...

ROMERO: (*Noticing blood on his robes.*) A searing fire hit my
        chest.

CELESTINA: You were shot by a sniper six days ago.

ROMERO: I was lying on the floor, staring up at the crucifix. You
        were standing over me! Celestina?

CELESTINA: Yes, Monseñor. (CELESTINA *a young nun, age
        thirty, appears from the shadows.*) The bullet entered your
        left breast. Parts of it broke up in your chest, causing
        heavy internal bleeding.

ROMERO: The last thing I remember was my violet vestment and
        white alb turning red.

CELESTINA: We carried you from the chapel to a panel truck out-
        side and drove you to the Policlínica Hospital five minutes
        away.

ROMERO: I was choking on my blood, strangling on my blood!

CELESTINA: The nun in the emergency room probed for a vein
        in your arm to start a transfusion, but your veins had

collapsed from lack of blood. A few minutes later you stopped gasping ... and died.

ROMERO: Why did it have to end this way?

CELESTINA: This is not the end, but the beginning.

ROMERO: What day is this?

CELESTINA: The day of your funeral. (*The sound of voices arguing are heard.*)

ROMERO: What are those voices?

CELESTINA: Voices of your mind, voices of the past.

ROMERO: What's happening to me!

CELESTINA: Think back, think back on all the choices you made in the three years of your ministry. (*Enter* GRANDE, REVELO *and* BARRERA *arguing.*)

ROMERO: My head! My mind feels like it's exploding! Why are they arguing, why are they shouting?

CELESTINA: The voices are getting louder, the sounds and feelings are pouring out.

ROMERO: (*Suddenly aware that they are skeletons.*) Barrera, Grande, Revelo! They look like they're dead!

CELESTINA: (*Stepping out of the shadows, her face a lightly drawn death mask.*) Yes, Monseñor. We're all dead or dying ... in one way or another.

ROMERO: Please, for the love of God! Stop!

CELESTINA: You must see, you must feel! Don't you remember? We were discussing your appointment as the new archbishop of San Salvador. I was there. (CELESTINA *leaves* ROMERO *and joins the others.*)

FEBRUARY 8, 1977. MEETING IN SANTA LUCÍA.

ROMERO: (*Warily approaching* GRANDE.) Rutilio? Rutilio! (GRANDE *and the others ignore him; he is not of their time or space.*)

GRANDE: Can we please call this meeting to order!

BARRERA: (*To* GRANDE.) I'm seriously thinking of moving to some other country where I will be able to do my pastoral work among the poor.

REVELO: You've got to give Romero a chance.

BARRERA: Romero is a throwback to the Middle Ages. He things you can solve malnutrition, ignorance and slum landlords through prayer and personal conversion.

REVELO: But prayer opens the gates to heaven.

GRANDE: What did Romero do that so offended you, Neto?

BARRERA: Remember when the military killed those students at the National University? Romero accused us of getting mixed up with the communists. He said that some of the students were terrorists.

REVELO: They admitted they were trained in Cuba.

BARRERA: (*Ignoring* REVELO.) After that, I seriously questioned whether I could, in all good conscience, celebrate the Eucharist with him.

GRANDE: I agree with Neto. I wouldn't want to see the good work in the poor barrios of the capital neglected.

REVELO: Yes, Neto, don't abandon your flock to the wolves.

BARRERA: Let me tell you something: I'll leave the priesthood if I have to.

GRANDE: Don't talk like that. You might be able to teach Romero a thing of two. You see, he's basically an introvert. When he has a problem, he shuts himself up in his room, prays, studies and then makes a decision.

BARRERA: Exactly, by Episcopal fiat. He refuses to listen to us.

GRANDE: But he is impeccably honest, with a tremendous capacity for work.

BARRERA: The nicest thing I can say about him is that he is the best of a bad lot.

REVELO: You know, Romero, even in the short period that he worked as auxiliary bishop, showed signs of having very delicate health. He's nervous. Notice how his hands shake. It's only a matter of time—he won't be able to handle the enormous amount of work.

BARRERA: Then what? We get someone more to your liking?

REVELO: Or yours!

GRANDE: Please! This is disrespectful towards our new archbishop. He has a great advantage over the others. He is honorable and faithful to his Christian commitment.

CELESTINA: I agree. We need to give him a chance to prove himself.

REVELO: Barrera, if he turns out to be another Herod, you can always go back to Galilee.

BARRERA: And you can hang yourself from a tree, Revelo!

REVELO: What do you mean by that? What do you mean by that!

GRANDE: Enough! Enough! Let us join together and pray that God guides our country in the midst of these difficult times. (*They join hands to pray silently.* GRANDE, REVELO *and* BARRERA *exit.*)

ROMERO: (*To* CELESTINA.) I can't believe some of them actually expected me to fail, and one of them actually wished it.

CELESTINA: It's because you were such a source of conflict and controversy. You see, Monseñor, it is not peace you came to bring, but a sword! (*Pointing to another area of the stage. Enter* CALAVERA SOLDADO *and* CALAVERA CAMPESINA. CELESTINA *and* ROMERO *exit.*)

AGUILARES—A RURAL COMMUNITY IN THE SALVADO-RAN COUNTRYSIDE—HALF OF THE POPULATION LIVES ON LESS THAN $10 A MONTH AND THREE-FIFTHS DOES NOT KNOW HOW TO READ OR WRITE.

SOLDADO: Micaela!

CAMPESINA: What do you want?

SOLDADO: I have a message for you.

CAMPESINA: A message? What kind of message?

SOLDADO: They say you are one of the ones who meets with Father Grande in the church, right?

CAMPESINA: Yes, I meet with Father Grande and others in the church.

SOLDADO: What does Father Grande teach you? What do you teach the others?

CAMPESINA: I don't teach anything. Everyone puts in their opinion and that's how we all learn.

SOLDADO: The truth is you take what you want out of the Bible and leave the rest behind, isn't that so?

CAMPESINA: Fidel, if you pick a mango, you eat what's inside and throw the skin away.

SOLDADO: It's not good for you to go to Father Grande's church. God says that when you want to pray, go to your house, shut the door, then pray.

CAMPESINA: But he also says, "What I whisper in your ear, preach it from the rooftops." Now, if you'll excuse me, I must be on my way.

SOLDADO: Micaela, listen to me, think of me as someone who cares about you.

CAMPESINA: You care about me?

SOLDADO: Yes, I do, and my advice to you is to stay away from Father Grande and his "red" church.

CAMPESINA: Thank you. Now, if you'll excuse me.

SOLDADO: Come on, you know the priest preaches subversive thoughts. For instance, he says, "if anyone has two shirts,

he must share with the man who has one. And the one
with something to eat must do the same."

CAMPESINA: That's what the Bible says, you're quoting from the
Bible.

SOLDADO: Bible or no Bible, you're in grave danger.

CAMPESINA: Of what!

SOLDADO: Of losing your life!

CAMPESINA: Ah, well, if that's it, then there's no problem.

SOLDADO: Why?

CAMPESINA: Because the Gospel tells us that he who seeks the
way of the Lord will die the same way he did!

SOLDADO: Damn it!

CAMPESINA: ¡Estúpido! Who do you think you are! You leave
Aguilares and come back with a uniform and a shiny
badge and you think you're a big man! (*She exits.*)

SOLDADO: You show some respect for this uniform. Smart ass!
Just wait and see!

*HALF OF 1 PERCENT OF ALL LANDOWNERS OWN 38
PERCENT OF THE ARABLE LAND, WHEREAS THE POORER
91 PERCENT OWN ONLY 23 PERCENT OF THE LAND.*

OLIGARCHY: (*Enter* MADAME OLIGARCHY *from the scaffolding area. She is heads and shoulders above everyone else.*)
Well, did you find out anything, Sargento?

SOLDADO: No, Señora. I have tape recordings of some sermons,
but it sounds just like the same old Christian crap.

OLIGARCHY: What do they say?

SOLDADO: The usual. They talk about the "Good News" and
how Jesus is the Father of all the people and, uh, not just
the, eh, rich.

OLIGARCHY: There you go!

SOLDADO: Well, everybody knows that!

OLIGARCHY: Shut up! It's subversive. No wonder the peasants
are up in arms. I want you to arrest the priest and throw
him in jail.

SOLDADO: On what charges, Señora?

OLIGARCHY: On the charges that I say so. Better yet, do away
with him completely.

SOLDADO: How?

OLIGARCHY: I don't know, I don't care. If my husband were
alive today, he'd know how to get rid of that meddlesome
priest.

SOLDADO: Look, here he comes now! (*Enter* GRANDE.)

ROMERO: (*Entering, intercepting* GRANDE. ROMERO'*s face is not as pale and deathly. As the play progresses he becomes more and more "alive."*) Father Grande! Don't go that way!

GRANDE: Romero! What brings you to the wilderness of Aguilares?

ROMERO: (*Leading* GRANDE *away from* OLIGARCHY *and* SOLDADO.) I wanted to talk to you.

GRANDE: Is something the matter? You're as pale as a ghost.

ROMERO: I'm tired.

GRANDE: What are you doing out here alone? Where's your entourage? You're the archbishop now, you deserve to travel in style.

ROMERO: I'm gathering a consensus of all the dioceses. What are the major problems? What can be done to alleviate them? What direction should we take?

GRANDE: I like that. You want to know if those of us in the caves can come down to the valley.

ROMERO: I hear you're having problems with the landowners.

GRANDE: Little by little the campesinos are overcoming their fatalism and realizing that hunger and the premature death of their children are not due to the will of God, but to the lust for profit of a few rich Salvadorans.

ROMERO: Come on, Rutilio, not all the rich are evil.

GRANDE: Evil no, but the landowners of Aguilares are still living in the nineteenth century.

ROMERO: They say you defended the campesinos' right to organize a union.

GRANDE: Yes, and for that they've been attacked by hired goons.

ROMERO: But the Constitution recognizes the right of assembly and association.

GRANDE: The Constitution is only for those who know how to read it.

ROMERO: When did all this bad blood begin, Rutilio?

GRANDE: With the coming of the conquistadores, Oscar! Seriously, though, the trouble began when the government built a hydroelectric power damn at Cerrón Grande.

ROMERO: That's progress, isn't it?

GRANDE: It only benefits the rich planters. The waters flooded small parcels of land belonging to the campesinos. A protest meeting was held at a local hacienda and a rich landowner, Regalado, was shot.

OLIGARCHY: (*Speaking up from the scaffolding, the* SOLDADO *beside her.*) Assassin! My husband was murdered in cold blood at his front door. In front of his wife and children!

GRANDE: (*Not aware of* OLIGARCHY.) There were conflicting reports of the shooting. The landowners seized on Regalado's death to start a smear campaign against the Jesuits.

OLIGARCHY: (*To audience.*) False prophets! They are to blame! My husband's blood is on their hands.

GRANDE: Antonio Navarro, the young priest who worked with me was arrested and detained incognito in the military barracks for over 48 hours.

SOLDADO: (*To* OLIGARCHY.) I suppose he's going to claim we beat him and tortured him with cattle prods?

ROMERO: Father Navarro was tortured!

GRANDE: Yes. I fear that soon the Gospel will not be allowed in our country. Only the bindings will arrive, nothing else, because the pages will be deemed subversive.

OLIGARCHY: (*Speaking directly to the audience.*) He says the Church is persecuted, but he doesn't talk about how his Church protects the Marxists who murdered my husband.

GRANDE: (*To the audience.*) If Jesus were to cross the border, they would arrest him. They would take him to different courts and accuse him of being a revolutionary, a foreign Jew.

OLIGARCHY: Communists!

GRANDE: Our Christ is not a silent Christ, a Christ of the cemetery. Ours is a young christ who died for his people at the age of thirty-three.

OLIGARCHY: (*Turning on* GRANDE *now.*) You bastard, you middle-class bastard! You're a traitor to your class!

GRANDE: (*Responding to* OLIGARCHY.) Would you crucify Christ again?

OLIGARCHY: (*To* SOLDADO.) Shoot him! Shoot him!

ROMERO: (*As* SOLDADO *draws his sidearm.*) Let's get away from here!

GRANDE: Let me go, I must face up to them!

OLIGARCHY: Come and meet your maker, priest!

ROMERO: (*Coming between the waring parties.*) No, no, no. Stop. There has to be a dialogue, we can't have any violence. (ROMERO *pushes* OLIGARCHY *and* SOLDADO *off stage.* GRANDE *exits as well.*)

CELESTINA: (*Entering.*) You were always the peacemaker, Monseñor.

ROMERO: It's not an easy role to play.

CELESTINA: You're trembling. Are you all right?

ROMERO: Yes. Perhaps they're right. I don't know how long I can keep doing this.

AGUILARES—THE KILLING FIELDS.

CELESTINA: It got worse, Monseñor, it got worse. The soldiers roared into Aguilares in armed cars, shooting into the air. (*As the* CALAVERAS *of Aguilares enter the scene.*) They accused the campesinos of helping the rebels. Juanito ran up the bell tower of the church to warn the people. They shot him dead. The soldiers searched every home, killed the pigs and chickens, and threw the grain on the floor. Everyone found with a bible or parish songbook was taken prisoner. Three young men are missing.

ROMERO: (*To the* CALAVERAS.) What were they looking for?

CAMPESINA: I don't know, arms, contraband. they urinated on the tabernacle, threw the hosts on the floor and defecated in the church.

CELESTINA: Where's Father Navarro?

CAMPESINA: They said they were going to drive him to the Guatemalan border and expel him from the country.

ROMERO: Who was the National Guard Commander? Do you know his name?

CAMPESINA: Manuel Sosa Jiménez, the San Carlos Garrison.

ROMERO: I'll go and talk to him right now.

CAMPESINA: Monseñor, you won't get any answers from him.

GRANDE: (*Entering.*) We just found the bodies of three young men by the roadside. Castrated—their genitals stuffed in their mouths!

ROMERO: Oh God!

CHORUS: (*From the group of* CALAVERAS.) When are we going to take some action? How long are we going to stand around and be slaughtered like sheep? Strike back! Assassins! Assassins! We want justice! Justice! Give us arms! Give us arms!

ROMERO: No, no! You can't go outside the law! You can't be like the beasts. This is not the way. We will demand justice in a court of law.

CAMPESINA: Monseñor! Listen to us. You don't know how many times we've complained to the civil authorities. They laugh in our faces!

ROMERO: I do know your problems. You mustn't lose faith.

CAMPESINA: No, excuse me, you don't know anything! Do you remember this morning when you asked for some food and I gave you a small tamal? You ate it, and a little later asked for more. You remember how we all looked at each other? No one said a thing, no one gave you anything.

ROMERO: Yes, I remember, but what does that ...

CAMPESINA: The reason no one gave you anything was because the soldiers destroyed it all. Most of us have not eaten at all today!

ROMERO: I'm sorry, forgive me.

CAMPESINA: And you claim to know our situation!

ROMERO: (*Embracing the* CAMPESINA, *embracing as many of them as he can.*) I promise to listen, watch and feel more. My children, my dear children. Please don't turn away from me! I love you, I love you all!

CELESTINA: Careful, your white robes are getting stained.

ROMERO: I want them stained. I want your sweat, earth, blood on me. I want to be marked with all of you!

CHORUS: (*The chorus of* CALAVERAS *files out,* ROMERO, GRANDE *and* CELESTINA *following behind them.*)

> We are the walking dead
> From the cane fields of Aguilares
> Our children suck sugar from stalks
> For want of nourishment.
>
> We are the walking dead
> From lack of food
> The dogs of the rich
> Are fed better than we
>
> We are the walking dead
> Rifles and helmets rise up
> Clattering teeth bark commands
> Filling the fields with skulls
>
> We are the walking dead
> Who can not read or write
> With no medicine for our ills
> And a hot sun beating down on us
>
> We are the walking dead, oh that
> Someday the church bells will peal

To announce the return of our spirits
From the dead

(*Up on the scaffolding, lights go up on el* SEÑOR CALAVERA
PRESIDENTE. *He is in his office applying shaving lotion on his
face and combing his hair.*)

*"WITH MONEY OR WITHOUT IT / I ALWAYS DO AS I
PLEASE / AND MY WORD IS THE LAW / BECAUSE I WILL
ALWAYS BE THE KING!"—POPULAR SONG.*

PRESIDENTE: (*Singing.*)

Con dinero o sin dinero
Hago siempre lo que quiero
Y mi palabra es la ley
Porque sigo siendo El Rey!

REPORTER: (*Enter blonde* AMERICAN CALAVERA RE-
PORTER. *Her Spanish is heavily accented.*) Buey-nos
dee-ass, See-noir Pres-ee-dent-ee!
PRESIDENTE: Señorita Smith, ¡bienvenida!
REPORTER: Thank you for granting me this interview.
PRESIDENTE: My pleasure. Hah, they didn't tell me you were so
young and good-looking. First of all, let me give you the
facts about my country. The official language is Spanish
. . .
REPORTER: Although I notice everyone speaks English quite well.
PRESIDENTE: Yes, I myself attended the University of Texas
in Austin. (*Makes "Hook 'em horns" sign with fingers.*)
Hook 'em horns! Now, the official currency is the Colon
. . .
REPORTER: But dollars will do quite nicely.
PRESIDENTE: Oh yes! (*Beat.*) We are a freely elected democratic
republic . . .
REPORTER: With a long tradition of electing military men pres-
idents, as you were last month.
PRESIDENTE: Yes, I hold the rank of general in the armed forces.
We pride ourselves on being the traditional defenders of
liberty. Now, our capital is San Salvador, from which the
fourteen departments are administered.
REPORTER: This Salvadorean businessman on the plane told me
a funny joke. He said, "They give the orders in San Salvador, but get the instructions from Washington."

PRESIDENTE: Yes, that's very funny. Now, our history is ...
REPORTER: Too much like the rest of Latin America. Or, as they
    say in Mexico, "far from God, but too close to the United
    States."
PRESIDENTE: (*Plainly irritated.*) You seem to know a great deal
    about my country. You said you were a free-lance writer.
    For what periodical?
REPORTER: *The New York Times.*
PRESIDENTE: (*Very receptive now.*) Oh well! What story are you
    researching?
REPORTER: It concerns the incident at Aguilares. Four campe-
    sinos and a priest named Father Alfonso Navarro were
    found shot to death.
PRESIDENTE: Listen, I have a very important luncheon to attend.
REPORTER: Now look, we're trying to present a balanced picture.
PRESIDENTE: No, I can't talk about the matter. It's still under
    investigation.
REPORTER: That's not the only story I'm here to write. I have
    other interests as well.
PRESIDENTE: (*Looking her over carefully.*) Have you had lunch
    yet? I know an excellent Basque restaurant nearby. (*Black-
    out on* PRESIDENTE'*s office. Lights up on the pulpit
    where* GRANDE *is eulogizing the dead of Aguilares.* RO-
    MERO *and* BARRERA *stand nearby.*)
GRANDE: They tell how a caravan, guided by a Bedouin, was
    desperate with thirst and sought water in the mirages of
    the desert. The guide kept saying, "No, not that way, this
    way." This happened several times, until one of the cara-
    van, his patience exhausted, killed the guide, who dying,
    kept pointing the way. Legend becomes reality: a priest,
    Father Alfonso Navarro, pierced with bullets, died par-
    doning his executioners.
BARRERA: (*To* ROMERO.) How are we going to respond to his
    outrage?
ROMERO: Let Father Grande finish his sermon!
GRANDE: All life is sacred—the life of Juanito who was climbing
    the bell tower, the life of the priest, as well as the lives
    of the soldiers who died in an ambush last week at the
    hands of the rebels. Violence is produced by all, not only
    by those who kill, but by those who urge others to kill.
BARRERA: How many more priests and peasants must die?
GRANDE: This is not the hour to be divided into two churches.
    It is the hour to feel ourselves one church that brings re-

demption not only beyond death, but here on earth! (*Applause.*)

ROMERO: You're not listening to what he's saying, are you, Barrera?

BARRERA: Words mean nothing, Monseñor, it's time for action. (*He exits.*)

GRANDE: (*Coming down from the pulpit.*) Barrera's heart is in the right place, it's his temper that needs cooling. Well, have you decided on a plan?

ROMERO: Well, some of the priests talked about only having one mass in the entire country next Sunday.

GRANDE: Good idea. I also think you should close down the Catholic schools for a few days.

ROMERO: Here comes Bishop Álvarez. (ÁLVAREZ, *an older man, ambles in.*) We're meeting right now to finalize our response. Why don't you join us?

GRANDE: But of course.

ÁLVAREZ: (*To* ROMERO.) Good afternoon, Excellency. I came as fast as my poor old legs could carry me after hearing of Navarro's death. Isn't it terrible!

ROMERO: He's buried and his soul is with God.

ÁLVAREZ: He's in a much better place than we are. (*Coldly, to* GRANDE.) Oh, hello, Father Grande.

GRANDE: Hello Bishop Álvarez.

ÁLVAREZ: Isn't it sad? We have to do something. These killings must stop!

ROMERO: I met with some of the priests in my diocese. They suggested having only one mass in the entire country next Sunday.

ÁLVAREZ: ¡Dios mío! What would that prove?

ROMERO: It will show, in a pastoral way, what expulsions and deaths of other priests can lead to.

GRANDE: We have to show the dangerous conditions that exist in our country today.

ÁLVAREZ: I just don't see how depriving the people of their Sunday mass will accomplish that. They need solace in their hour of grief.

GRANDE: I feel that we should also close down the Catholic schools for a few days.

ÁLVAREZ: Close the schools? What for?

GRANDE: So they'll come clean regarding Father Navarro's murder.

ÁLVAREZ: The Catholic schools killed Father Navarro!

GRANDE: No, no, no. Each student could be sent home with a discussion guide. That would make everyone, including the killers, think about the effects of Navarro's death.

ROMERO: Moral persuasion.

ÁLVAREZ: Sounds like a show of power. Why deprive the students of their education and risk angering their parents? What's going to be in this discussion guide?

GRANDE: Questions regarding the persecution of priests.

ÁLVAREZ: Persecution! There is no persecuted Church. There are only some sons of the Church, wanting to serve God, who lost themselves in the dusky woods.

GRANDE: Are you referring to Navarro?

ALVAREZ: No, no, no. Navarro was a fine priest. It's terrible what happened to him. Something must be done! But your proposals seem counter-productive to me.

ROMERO: Well, what do you suggest?

ÁLVAREZ: I don't know, a special mass perhaps.

GRANDE: Another issue comes to mind. Should the Church be seen supporting the government by attending official functions?

ÁLVAREZ: No, now you're going too far. This is truly provocative.

ROMERO: I'm not sure I agree with that either. Why make the situation worse? I want the government to take us into account without surrendering our independence.

ÁLVAREZ: Exactly. If we respect the civil authorities, they will respect us.

GRANDE: But don't you think we should take a firm stand? It's not only priests who are being expelled from the country and killed, but also campesinos, workers, students, teachers.

ÁLVAREZ: No! I say let us be of one mind with the Church, the Pope and with our republic. We need to give El Señor Presidente the warmth of our virtue and charity, as St. Peter did.

ROMERO: I'm going to see the president this afternoon. He has to promise that he'll put an end to the expulsion of priests and bring Navarro's killers to trial. Agreed?

ÁLVAREZ: (*As* GRANDE *nods in agreement.*) I don't know ...

ROMERO: So, are we ready to vote?

ÁLVAREZ: I make a motion that we postpone this for further consideration.

GRANDE: We can't put this off much longer.

ÁLVAREZ: I see you have me outnumbered!

ROMERO: We're only voting on the mass and school issue. We'll leave the topic of cooperating with the government for later.

ÁLVAREZ: Very well, I vote "no" to everything! (*They exit. The focus shifts to the presidente's office where he is conversing with* MADAME OLIGARCHY.)

OLIGARCHY: You machos are such suckers for las gringas. Be careful you don't reveal more than you should. She could be a spy.

PRESIDENTE: I'll have to cancel the rest of my afternoon appointments.

OLIGARCHY: (*Looking out the window.*) Afraid not, dear. Here comes the archbishop with his black robes flapping in the breeze.

PRESIDENTE: I'll go out the back way. You can reach me at the country club.

OLIGARCHY: No, I think we better hear what his Excellency has to say.

PRESIDENTE: Oh shit. Next time you get to play the presidente. (*Barking an order into the intercom, as* OLIGARCHY *hides behind a curtain.*) Let the archbishop in. (*To himself.*) Bastard, probably sleeps with the nuns.

ROMERO: (*Entering.*) Thank you for seeing me so promptly, Señor Presidente.

PRESIDENTE: Your Excellency, my office is open to you twenty-four hours per day. What's on your mind?

ROMERO: I came to inquire as to the progress in the investigation of the death of Father Navarro and the four campesinos of Aguilares.

PRESIDENTE: The investigation is proceeding. I can assure you that in due time we will discover the culprits and apply the full rigor of the law.

ROMERO: But we know who did it. It was the San Carlos Garrison.

PRESIDENTE: Hearsay! My intelligence tells me of a wave of anti-social actions that seek to disrupt the public order—with the purpose of blaming the government.

ROMERO: We don't know the names of the soldiers, but their commander is Manuel Sosa Jiménez.

PRESIDENTE: The prime minister's nephew?

ROMERO: Yes, the prime minister's nephew. He's been seen dining and attending social functions here in the capital.

PRESIDENTE: Oh, I thought he was under house arrest. All I
can say at this time is that the investigation is proceeding. I promise to personally inform you the instant I hear
anything. Now, if you'll excuse me, I have an urgent, eh,
affair of state. (ROMERO *hands him a list.*) What's this?

ROMERO: A list of disappeared persons. We are hearing many
complaints of arbitrary arrests.

PRESIDENTE: Look, many of the so-called "disappeared" are
merely awaiting trial. As for the arrests, remember that
parts of our beloved Fatherland are occupied by foreign
mercenaries who are disturbing the public order.

ROMERO: We are also seeing many signs of torture.

PRESIDENTE: You, personally?

ROMERO: Yes, torture and rape.

PRESIDENTE: Do you want me to show you the mutilated bodies
of our soldiers in the city morgue! This is war, Bishop!

ROMERO: I don't deny that many of the rebels are guilty of excesses. I wish all the violence would end.

PRESIDENTE: Well, instruct your priests to stop instigating class
struggle. They only chastise the rich. Tell the poor to stop
breaking the laws.

ROMERO: I only wish the rich would share some of their wealth
with the poor.

PRESIDENTE: They should be thankful for what they have.
(*Beat.*) Bishop, let's be frank; there are many ways you
and I can calm the troubled waters.

ROMERO: I agree. We can start by bringing back the expelled
priests. Their pastoral work is sorely missed.

PRESIDENTE: Yes, of course. I'm willing to make concessions.
You know, my Inauguration is next week. We've sent
several invitations to the Chancellery and you haven't
replied.

ROMERO: Mr. Presidente, after much soul searching I have decided that I cannot attend any official government functions until the perpetrators of the Aguilares massacre are
brought to justice.

PRESIDENTE: You act as if I personally pulled the trigger! What
about the kidnapping of my foreign minister, Mauricio
Borgonovo? Why don't you say anything about him at
your masses?

ROMERO: We did broadcast an appeal on the Catholic radio. But
if the captivity of a prominent person is so horrible, isn't

the disappearance of any ordinary citizen in the prisons equally odious?

PRESIDENTE: Let's make a deal. I promise a hands-off policy in the conduct of church affairs, if you keep the tradition of attending my presidential Inauguration next week.

ROMERO: You want me to bless your Inauguration?

PRESIDENTE: It would be a great honor.

ROMERO: In return, you'll promise to cease the harassment of priests, allow the exiles to return and find Father Navarro's killers?

PRESIDENTE: Yes. I give you my solemn word as a Christian and an officer!

ROMERO: You must also look into the disappeared persons. I want action, not promises.

PRESIDENTE: (*Showing* ROMERO *out the door.*) You don't know what this means to me. I am confident that we shall make justice shine forth and remedy the ills that plague our beloved Fatherland.

ROMERO: God wish it so.

PRESIDENTE: (*Talking into the intercom.*) Send in the reporter. (OLIGARCHY *appears from behind curtain.*)

OLIGARCHY: He's not going to attend your Inauguration.

PRESIDENTE: Why not?

OLIGARCHY: He's not following the script.

PRESIDENTE: For Christ sake, you recommended him to Rome.

OLIGARCHY: I know.

PRESIDENTE: Well then, what's the problem?

OLIGARCHY: I didn't realize he had so much principle. (*They exit.*)

SOLDADO: (*Enter* CAMPESINA, *followed by* SOLDADO.) Micaela, I tell you, I didn't know anything about the Aguilares raid. I wasn't there.

CAMPESINA: Those were your drinking buddies. We know you go whoring and drinking with them.

SOLDADO: Am I my brother's keeper?

CAMPESINA: Don't give me that. You practically wear the same uniform. Get away from me, you're drunk!

SOLDADO: Micaela. I'm just trying to warn you! (*Trying to grab her.*)

CAMPESINA: Let go of me, Fidel!

SOLDADO: (*As they struggle.*) You don't understand, you're in danger.

CAMPESINA: (*Slapping* SOLDADO.) Get your hands off me!

SOLDADO: (*Thrusting her to the ground.*) What are you going to do, eh? (*Throwing himself on top of her.*) There's no one here but you and me! (*Trying to kiss her.*)

CAMPESINA: You bastard!

SOLDADO: You see what happened to the priest. The same thing can happen to you! Are you going to listen to me now!

CAMPESINA: All right, I'm listening!

SOLDADO: You act so high and mighty! Don't tell me you're not afraid.

CAMPESINA: I'm afraid. I'm only human. What about you? Aren't you afraid your own people will turn on you?

SOLDADO: Soldiers aren't afraid of death. We live death.

CAMPESINA: Your job deals with death. But you don't know anything about what comes after death.

SOLDADO: What comes after death?

CAMPESINA: Resurrection!

SOLDADO: Resurrection! (*Trying to disrobe her.*) Aren't you afraid of this, eh, eh?

CAMPESINA: The only thing I'm afraid of is being far from God! (*This stops him.*)

SOLDADO: (*Rising, in disgust.*) You don't understand why I'm telling you this, to stop going to that church.

CAMPESINA: No, I don't.

SOLDADO: Because I love you, that's why!

CAMPESINA: You have a strange way of showing your love.

SOLDADO: More and more people are going to get killed.

CAMPESINA: If what you say is true, you've certainly mixed things up for me.

SOLDADO: Why?

CAMPESINA: Well, you say you're doing this out of love for me. Not to go to church. While someone else who loves me tells me just the opposite.

SOLDADO: And just who the hell is that?

CAMPESINA: Why, Jesus Christ!

GRANDE: (*Entering.*) What's happening here!

SOLDADO: (*Letting* CAMPESINA *get up.*) Nothing, priest! You just keep out of this.

GRANDE: (*To* CAMPESINA.) Are you all right?

CAMPESINA: Yes. (*The* SOLDADO *turns on his heel and exits.*) He was drunk. (*Dusting herself off.*)

GRANDE: Did he hurt you?

CAMPESINA: No. But I'm going to kill him if he does it again!

GRANDE: Micaela, that won't solve matters. Remember that the power of non-violence is much stronger than violence because it carries the power of love and the conviction that we are all brothers.

CAMPESINA: But how often must we turn the other cheek?

GRANDE: Remember when Anna was interrogating Jesus and a policeman slapped our Lord in the face? Christ turned to his tormentor and protested: "Why do you strike me? If I have done wrong, tell me what it is that I did. But if I have not done wrong, then why do you strike me?"

CAMPESINA: In other words, speak out, defend yourself, demand justice!

GRANDE: The Lord said, "Thou shall not kill," but He also said, "Thou shall not commit suicide!" (*They exit.*)

OLIGARCHY: (*At the* PRESIDENTE's *office with* BISHOP ÁLVAREZ.) They found the foreign minister's body. Shot in the head, just like my husband. The funeral mass will be tomorrow with the Presidente and the entire cabinet.

ÁLVAREZ: He's in a better place than we are. (*Comforting her.*) All the bishops will be there as well.

OLIGARCHY: Even Romero?

ÁLVAREZ: Why, of course. Why do you ask?

OLIGARCHY: He doesn't attend "official functions" any more.

ÁLVAREZ: Oh, this is different.

OLIGARCHY: I want to tell you, we're very displeased with Monseñor Romero.

ÁLVAREZ: It's not his fault. He's too good, too much a man of prayer and sacrifice, to slip into the errors that are being committed.

OLIGARCHY: Well then, his mind is being poisoned by some of his communist priests.

ÁLVAREZ: Perhaps—some of the Jesuits should have stayed in their schools for the sons of the rich and not gotten involved in rural parishes. I'm going to have the Papal Nuncio talk to him.

OLIGARCHY: The venom is spreading. Do you know that one of your priests is being questioned regarding the prime minister's abduction.

ALVAREZ: No! Who?

OLIGARCHY: Father Rutilio Grande.

ÁLVAREZ: Why, that's preposterous. Father Grande may be liberal, but he wouldn't get mixed up in something like that.

OLIGARCHY: A search of his quarters revealed subversive liter-
ature. Worse yet, he's been inciting the campesinos to
violence!
ÁLVAREZ: No, I don't believe it!
OLIGARCHY: And don't forget, he was questioned in the murder
of my husband!
ÁLVAREZ: He had nothing to do with it!
OLIGARCHY: Where are you training these bastards, in Cuba!
ÁLVAREZ: I'll see that Father Grande is transferred immediately.
OLIGARCHY: Yes, you do that, right away! (*They exit.*)

  *BE A PATRIOT, KILL A PRIEST!—WHITE WARRIORS
UNION, JULY 20, 1977.*

GRANDE: (*Preaching at the pulpit.*) We come to share at this table
which is a symbol of our brotherhood, a table with a chair
and a plate for each person.
DEATH SQUAD: (*With black hood over his head, reading a procla-
mation.*) War Order No. 6, San Salvador. The Supreme
Command of the White Warriors Union. All Jesuits without exception must leave the country forever within thirty
days of this date.
GRANDE: But there are groups of Cains in our family, here in this
country. And Cain is an abortion of the plan of God. And
these Cains cry out, "I bought half of El Salvador with my
money, and that gives me certain rights! You cannot argue
with that! My word is law because I paid for the right!"
DEATH SQUAD: The religious orders and priests who are not
agents of international communism have nothing to fear
and can continue their work in complete tranquility. Our
struggle is not against the Church but against the Jesuit
guerrillas.
GRANDE: The Father has sent me to bring the good news to the
poor, to proclaim liberty to captives and give sight to the
blind, to set the oppressed free.
DEATH SQUAD: If our order is not obeyed within the indicated
time, the immediate and systematic execution of all Jesuits who remain in the country will proceed!
GRANDE: (*As* SOLDADO CALAVERAS *march up to the pulpit
and surround* GRANDE.) The Jesuits will stay in El Salvador. We will not leave unless we are expelled or physically eliminated. Christian power is far stronger than a
two-edged sword because it is based on the teachings of

Jesus Christ. It is a power that neither money nor guns can destroy.

DEATH SQUAD: (*As an ALTAR BOY and an OLD MAN join GRANDE to assist in the mass.*) Furthermore, all associates of the Jesuits are warned that installations and places frequented by them will be considered military targets. We will not be responsible for the death of third persons as a consequence of our operations.

GRANDE: Remember my words! If a person is in extreme necessity, he has the right to take from the riches of others what he himself needs! (*The SOLDIERS lead GRANDE up to the cross and tie him to it.*) Feed the man dying of hunger, because if you have not fed him, you have murdered him.

DEATH SQUAD: The deadline is July 20, 1977. Long live the Commandoes of Liberty! War to the death with International Communism! The Fatherland to Power! White Warrior Union! (*The SOLDADOS execute GRANDE, the ALTAR BOY, and the OLD MAN. DEATH SQUAD and SOLDADOS exit as the Cathedral fills with mourners. GRANDE's body is taken down from the cross and all three corpses are covered with blood stained sheets.*)

CHORUS: (*Singing.*) De colores, de colores se visten los campos en la primavera. (*Repeat.*) Y por eso los grandes amores de muchos colores me gustan a mí. (*REPEAT.*)

ROMERO: (*During this time ROMERO has put on his mitre and bishop's robes to preach from the same pulpit that GRANDE spoke.*) Father Grande's death is a message for all of us who remain on this pilgrimage called life. The liberation that he preached was a liberation based on faith. That is the reason Father Grande died. Like him, the Church is inspired by love and rejects hatred. Who knows if the murderers that have now fallen into excommunication are listening to a radio in their hideout. We want to tell you, murderous brethren, that we love you and ask of God repentance for your crimes! The Church is not able to hate and has no enemies. Its only enemies are those who want to declare themselves so. But the Church loves and dies, like Father Grande, saying with his last breath, "Father, forgive them, they know not what they do!" (*All the mourners, except for SISTER CELESTINA, disperse.*)

CELESTINA: You were very close to Father Grande, weren't you?

ROMERO: (*Looking at GRANDE's body.*) He was very present

at peak moments in my life. Rutilio had been master of ceremonies at my Episcopal ordination.

CELESTINA: What effect did his ministry have on you?

ROMERO: His words rang true to my ears. They cleared a straight path, filling in every ravine and mountain, straightening the corners and making the rugged way smooth. His death was like a call from God. I asked myself, how is it that such a good, honest man was murdered? At that moment I knew that I myself might have to take the same path some day. You might say I was baptized in his blood! (*Blackout.*)

ACT TWO

The Cathedral. The bodies of GRANDE *and the two* CAMPE-SINOS *are gone.*

"I, THE LORD, HAVE CALLED YOU WITH RIGHTEOUS PURPOSE AND TAKEN YOU BY THE HAND; I HAVE FORMED YOU, AND APPOINTED YOU TO BE LIGHT TO ALL PEO-PLES, A BEACON FOR THE NATIONS, TO OPEN EYES THAT ARE BLIND, TO BRING CAPTIVES OUT OF PRISON, OUT OF THE DUNGEONS WHERE THEY LIE IN DARKNESS—" ISA-IAH 42:1–8.

BARRERA: (*Entering with* ROMERO *and* CELESTINA.) How many more people and priests must die?

CELESTINA: What do you suggest?

BARRERA: It's time we sided with the mass movements and followed their lead.

ROMERO: Didn't you listen to my sermon? I said that liberation must not be thought of in a strictly materialistic way.

BARRERA: You mean "a better life in the hereafter?"

ROMERO: I was talking about the here and now.

BARRERA: The question is: How are we going to pressure the government into bringing the killers of Father Grande and the others to trial?

CELESTINA: Neto, is that all you're looking for—any eye for an eye?

ROMERO: Father Grande's death will not have been in vain. I will show El Señor Presidente that we will no longer tolerate their hands-off attitude in regards to the death squads.

BARRERA: But excommunicating them isn't going to work!

CELESTINA: What do you want to do, Neto, start a crusade?

BARRERA: The people have the right to defend themselves against the institutionalized violence of the state.

ROMERO: What do you mean by "institutionalized violence?"

BARRERA: The kind of violence that kills people slowly, by denying them food, medicine, education, a roof over their heads.

CELESTINA That kind of theology threatens the teachings of the Church.

BARRERA: No, only the state! When Christ preached the liberation of Israel, he said, "Give unto Caesar what is Caesar's, but give unto God what is God's." He meant that the wealth of Israel must not be squandered on a foreign host. Our national resources are going into the hands of a few rich Salvadorans and their imperialist financiers abroad.

CELESTINA: Revelo's right, you are a Zealot!

BARRERA: And so was Simon. And when Jesus first proclaimed his message, it was in Galilee, a stronghold of Zealotism.

CELESTINA: What do you want to do, Neto? Start another Vietnam in Central America and bring the Americans down on us?

BARRERA: Don't you see, they're already here! We have to stop turning the other cheek.

ROMERO: Do you think that was cowardly?

CELESTINA: (*To* BARRERA, *who does not answer* ROMERO.) Neto, you're in danger of losing your Christian soul!

ROMERO: Far from being cowardly or passive, the advice of the Gospel to turn the other cheek to an unjust aggressor is the showing of great moral force that leaves the assailant overcome and humiliated.

BARRERA: Do you want the lambs to lie down with the lions so they can be devoured?

ROMERO: No! But bombing bridges, destroying crops and highjacking buses isn't my idea of a revolutionary posture!

BARRERA: (*Both* BARRERA *and* CELESTINA *are taken back, as this is the first time* ROMERO *has shown any real anger.*) What are we to do then?

ROMERO: I need to make sure that there is a Christian presence in the union movement at Aguilares now that Father Grande is gone. Would you like to take his place?

BARRERA: I would like that very much.

ROMERO: But as their pastor, you must give them advice that will steer them away from danger. Any kind of violence is dangerous, do you understand?

BARRERA: Yes, Monseñor.

ROMERO: As for the deaths of our priests and parishioners, I am going to formulate a strong response to the government. I promise that justice will be done. Go now, we both have a great deal of work to do. (*Exit* ROMERO.)

CELESTINA: (*To* BARRERA.) So, what do you think?

BARRERA: He's changed considerably from the man who used to frown upon young priests appearing without cassocks. He even disapproved of nuns and priests socializing.

CELESTINA: He's no longer the petty bourgeois whose wealthy friends in the capital raised money for his ordination as bishop.

BARRERA: No, but the real test of his mettle will come soon, when the Pharisees and Romans start screaming for his head. (*They exit.*)

PRESIDENTE: (*At his office with* OLIGARCHY, *waving a newspaper.*) How dare he attack our trial lawyers and justices in public?

OLIGARCHY: (*Grabbing the paper and reading.*) Let me see. He said that there are "anomalies in the procedures of the court ... where the judge does not allow lawyers to enter with their defendants, while the Guardia Nacional is allowed to be present and intimidate the accused, who often bear evident signs of torture."

PRESIDENTE: This is blatant interference in our affairs.

OLIGARCHY: (*Continuing to read.*) "A judge who does not report signs of torture is not a just judge in the eyes of the accused!"

PRESIDENTE: In his sermons—he said that certain judges sell themselves—it even came out on the radio!

OLIGARCHY: We have to draft a strong response.

PRESIDENTE: (*Dictating into a tape recorder.*) Absolutely! To His Excellency, the Archbishop of San Salvador. Where the hell do you get off talking that kind of crap!

OLIGARCHY: (*Taking over.*) We most respectfully beg your Excellency to identify by name the "venal judges" to whom you referred in your sermon and which was broadcast by radio station YSAX, in order to proceed to trial and judgment if your accusation should prove correct.

PRESIDENTE: Are you serious? You want him to name the corrupt judges!

OLIGARCHY: He won't dare name them. I'm going to send this statement to all the media.

PRESIDENTE: But what if he does? My brother-in-law is a judge.

OLIGARCHY: The burden of proof will be on Romero. We'll put him on trial. In our courts. He'll be dragged into a messy case and expose himself to charges of slander, or contempt of court.

PRESIDENTE: And if he says nothing?

OLIGARCHY: He backs down and loses face. We'll call him a liar, a coward. Either way, he loses.

PRESIDENTE: Wonderful! I hope he takes the bait!

ROMERO: (*Appearing at the pulpit.*) The Presidente begs me most respectfully to identify by name the venal judges to whom I referred in my homily last Sunday. I am not a jurist, but a pastor, who is simply pointing out the existence of an institutional wrong that needs mending. But even more serious than venality is the Supreme Court's absolute contempt for the Salvadoran Constitution. Please, Señor Presidente, hear this in the spirit of constructive criticism and not as a malicious desire to defame. The people must once again have faith in our system of justice. I am saying this as my duty as pastor, a duty placed on me by the Gospel, for which I am ready to face trial and prison if need be. (*Applause.*)

ÁLVAREZ: (*Who has now joined* PRESIDENTE *and* OLIGARCHY.) Do you see what you've done! You've driven him to this!

ROMERO: I wish to thank all the lawyers and law students who told me they too shared the Church's concern for justice.

PRESIDENTE: I say we arrest him!

ROMERO: The Church of the Holy Spirit has proclaimed from the distant time of the prophet Isaiah—and today repeats with the renewed youth of this Pentecost—Peace can only be the product of Justice! (*Applause.*)

OLIGARCHY: He's gone mad, truly mad.

ÁLVAREZ: You know, he was once hospitalized for nervous tension. He nearly had a nervous breakdown.

PRESIDENTE: I say we place him on trial at once!

OLIGARCHY: (*Turning on* PRESIDENTE.) No! We can't do that! Do you want to make a martyr of him! (*The three exit.*)

CELESTINA: (*Entering, crossing to* ROMERO.) Monseñor, the Papal Nuncio is here from Guatemala to see you!

ROMERO: I was afraid of that. Things aren't going very well. I've buried two of my most respected priests and tensions with the presidente are at a new high.

CELESTINA: Don't despair. Many of the younger clergy who received you with displeasure now support you wholeheartedly. Most importantly, the common people are returning to church in droves to hear you.

ROMERO: But I've lost ground with the ruling class, some of whom are obviously complaining to the hierarchy. Perhaps I need to go to Rome to explain my side of the story.

CELESTINA: Like St. Paul who went to explain his work to the apostles? I pray you won't have as much trouble as he did.

ROMERO: That's what I like about you, Sister Celestina, there's such a Biblical quality about your speech! Show his Excellency in. And bring us some of that Portuguese sherry. If I get him to unwind, he won't be so irascible. (*Enter* PAPAL NUNCIO, *an old grey-haired* CALAVERA *with a cane.* ROMERO *embraces him warmly.*) Hah, Fidencio! We're so glad you came to visit us in the midst of your busy schedule.

NUNCIO: It is my duty as Papal Nuncio to keep in touch with our Salvadorean clergy.

ROMERO: Would you like a glass of sherry? (*As* CELESTINA *brings it in, serving both of them.*)

NUNCIO: Thank you, Sister. (*Watching her leave.*) Is it my imagination, or are the nuns getting prettier these days? Oscar, Oscar, Oscar. Salud! (*Toasting him.*) Just what I need to cure this splitting headache. Do you know how I got this headache, Oscar?

ROMERO: Let me guess. Certain young priests organizing the campesinos and urban shantytown dwellers into Christian Base Communities?

NUNCIO: Yes, yes, yes. Those groups of laity who get together to read the Bible. Go on.

ROMERO: They only assist the poor in claiming the basic rights due to them as children of God: adequate nutrition, a decent living wage, health care.

NUNCIO: (*Holding his head.*) Go on.

ROMERO: Perhaps your headache began with my predecessor, Monseñor Chávez, who initiated the application of the

principles of the Second Vatican Council and Medellín
and whose policies I am merely continuing.

NUNCIO: Yes, yes, yes. I know all about the "preferential option
for the poor" and all that other rhetoric.

ROMERO: Fidencio, the priests don't do this out of any revolutionary posture. They have merely opened cooperatives,
medical clinics and farmworker unions.

NUNCIO: Some very prominent people have been abducted and
murdered.

ROMERO: Our Christian communities reject violence.

NUNCIO: I think you're being very naive. (*Showing an empty
glass.*) Please. (*As* ROMERO *fills his glass.*) I'll be frank
with you, Oscar, many people both here and abroad find
your actions irresponsible, imprudent and inconsistent
with Church teachings.

ROMERO: I bear full responsibility. All my decisions came about
after long and studied consultations with my clergy.

NUNCIO: That's just it! You mustn't let them lead you around
by the nose. You're the archbishop! What's happening to
you, Oscar? You're pushing the Church down the road to
confrontation with the state! You used to be so ...

ROMERO: Safe. Quiet? Cowardly!

NUNCIO: No, you were prudent, sensible! You can't deny that
some of your priests are hot heads and rabble rousers?

ROMERO: Perhaps a few. But my way is to keep communications
open with them while indicating my displeasure at their
involvement.

NUNCIO: Oscar, you're playing into the hands of the communists!

ROMERO: No, we are neither with the left, nor with the right.

NUNCIO: Haven't some of your priests taken up arms?

ROMERO: Fidencio! What are you saying? The Church is a voice
of moderation.

NUNCIO: I've heard some strange stories, wild rumors. You must
moderate your position in regards to the government, do
you hear me! I will not have you galloping full tilt down
the road to Armageddon!! Rome demands your obedi-
ence!

ROMERO: I'll take your words into deepest consideration, Fidencio.

NUNCIO: (*Becoming friendly again.*) Oscar, Oscar. Remember
those good times we had in Rome? All that good wine
and Italian food, the theaters, the circus, the clowns with
their earthy proletarian humor. What if I arranged for

you to work in Rome again! (ROMERO *shakes his head
"no."*) No?

ROMERO: I cannot leave my people.

NUNCIO: Your people? Your people! Who do you think you are,
Oscar, Jesus Christ? (*Fade on the above.*)

*"KILL THE DOG, AND YOU GET RID OF THE RABIES"—
SALVADORAN PROVERB.*

REPORTER: (*Entering with* MAJOR D'ABUSSION *at a fashion-
able sidewalk cafe.*) So, you're the famous Major Roberto
D'Abussion?

MAJOR: In the flesh. (*Ordering a drink from an imaginary waiter.*)
Two whiskeys.

REPORTER: And so charming too!

MAJOR: Señorita, you flatter me.

REPORTER: Well, what do you have to say for yourself? I have
a story to file.

MAJOR: We have a saying here in my country, "muerto el perro,
se acabó la rabia."

REPORTER: Dead the dog and the rabies are done?

MAJOR: Kill the dog, and you get rid of the rabies. That's what
happened in 1932. The communists stirred up the Indians
and other malcontents who slaughtered plantation owners
and their entire families. The people formed a Guardia
Civil to help out the army and within a few weeks 50,000
reds were dead.

REPORTER: How do you know the uprising was communist inspired?

MAJOR: The rebellion was led by a misguided student named
Farabundo Martí. The terrorists now call themselves the
Farabundo Martí Liberation Front. It's a fact that in the
1930's Martí trained with Sandino in Nicaragua.

REPORTER: You mean, Augusto Sandino, as in the Sandinistas?

MAJOR: Exactly. I tell you, unless we stop them now, the entire region from Panama to Guatemala will turn red with
blood. And Southern Mexico, with its oil, is next.

REPORTER: So that's why we're getting so many Central American refugees?

MAJOR: San Salvador is only a few days drive from Texas. And
unless your country gives us the funds to fight and pacify
the countryside, swarms of illegal aliens will be climbing
your fences.

REPORTER: What's your opinion of Archbishop Romero?

MAJOR: Never in the whole history of mankind have you seen such a poor persecuted church. Those poor little lambs with horns and razor sharp claws. Can't you just see the tears rolling down the cheeks of the statues of Jesus and Mary?

REPORTER: You think he's a fraud?

MAJOR: A veritable hypocrite who laughs behind our backs. He goes around Europe campaigning for the Nobel Peace Prize—talking about how the rich should give up their wealth. But look at the church! Why don't they divide their wealth and give it to the beggars on the streets?

REPORTER: Where does the concept of "liberation theology" come from?

MAJOR: Supposedly some documents from a church conference where a certain group of bishops, most certainly in the wrong business, decided the spiritual orientation of man is very boring. Thus they thrust themselves into wordly affairs.

REPORTER: That's where the guerrilla priests come from?

MAJOR: Exactly. The only problem is that in the waters in which they swim live fishes of another kind, like those of the KGB, who can swallow them whole.

REPORTER: May I quote you on that? This is going to make great copy back in the States.

MAJOR: Certainly. Now, where do you want to go for dinner? I know of an excellent Mexican restaurant. (MAJOR *pays the bill and they both exit.*)

CELESTINA: (*At the Cathedral.* CELESTINA, REVELO, ÁLVAREZ *and* ROMERO.) My God! Dear God! They've shot Neto Barrera!

ROMERO: Are you certain?

CELESTINA: Yes, it's on all the newscasts and over the radio. They said he died in a shootout with the National Guard!

ROMERO: Impossible, impossible. There must be some mistake.

REVELO: They say that Father Barrera was one of four members of the Popular Liberation Forces who died in a violent five hour gun battle.

CELESTINA: At least part of the government story is clearly a lie. They claim all the guerrillas died, but witnesses saw one man who surrendered with his hands in the air. Television reporters even interviewed him.

ÁLVAREZ: Barrera died with a gun in his hand.

CELESTINA: This is not the first time that the security forces have staged a fake shoot-out and planted a gun in someone's hand.

ÁLVAREZ: But even the guerrillas are claiming that Barrera was a full-fledged member, with the nom de guerre, "Felipe."

ROMERO: If this is true, then I am sorely grieved.

CELESTINA: (*To the men.*) Do you see your reaction? You deplore the murders of Grande and Navarro, but there's no way you can defend a church that held within its bosom a radical like Barrera!

REVELO: (*Ignoring* CELESTINA.) The question now is what do we do with the immediate problem of Barrera's funeral?

ÁLVAREZ: We can't even think of presiding at it. It is already a dark stain on the Church. I don't even think he can be buried as a priest.

CELESTINA: You've already condemned him without knowing all the facts!

REVELO: Why not hand him over to his family and let them bury Barrera alone in the little village where he came from?

CELESTINA: Listen to me! In the first place, we aren't sure how Neto died. In the second place, even if he did die with a pistol in his hand, it wasn't because of any selfish interest. He lived and died because of his love for the people. The least the Church can do is give him a Christian burial as a priest of the Church.

ROMERO: I really don't know how Father Barrera died. If he did belong to the guerrillas, we did not know or approve of it. Let this be a warning to all. The archdiocese's policy is clear. Any priest who involves himself with a violent group does a disservice to the Church and the cause of the poor. Let us go now and prepare for the funeral.

ÁLVAREZ: Wait a minute! You trusted Barrera, you gambled on his integrity, and he betrayed you!

REVELO: He was a bad apple, be thankful he can no longer contaminate others.

ROMERO: Do you think that Barrera's mother, without questioning the circumstances, will be next to the body of her son at the funeral?

ÁLVAREZ: But it will appear as if you were condoning the guerrilla priests!

ROMERO: No! I, as his bishop, must be next to him in death as he was in life! (ROMERO *starts off as* ÁLVAREZ *and*

REVELO *conspire in whispers*.) Father Revelo—are you coming with me?

REVELO: Coming, Monseñor!

ÁLVAREZ: (*Fuming with anger*.) Revelo, try and talk some sense into him! (*Exit* REVELO *with* ROMERO.) Sister Celestina, may I have a word with you, please?

CELESTINA: Yes, Bishop Álvarez.

ÁLVAREZ: Have you noticed anything different about Monseñor Romero lately—His health, attitude?

CELESTINA: Well, I notice he doesn't get sick anymore, not even a cold. It's as though the work has made him stronger.

ÁLVAREZ: (*Sarcastically*.) It must be a miracle of grace.

CELESTINA: It must be. When he first started working his hands would shake when he drank coffee. Now he's as steady as a rock. He seems to mature and grow stronger with each confrontation.

ÁLVAREZ: He's changed that much in two years?

CELESTINA: Oh yes! At his age most men are rigid and their psychological patterns already formed. Especially people in positions of authority.

ÁLVAREZ: Did you major in sociology at the university or something?

CELESTINA: No, sir. I'm talking about the spiritual growth I have observed in Monseñor Romero. It's as though he's driven by the God of Change, by a new and different sense of what it means to be a Christian.

ÁLVAREZ: The God of Change! The God of Change you say! (*They exit*.)

ROME—THE TOMB OF ST. PETER.

REVELO: (*Entering with* ROMERO.) How did the Pope receive you?

ROMERO: Very coldly.

REVELO: I was praying for you here at the tomb of St. Peter.

ROMERO: He doesn't understand our pastoral work. He is even considering the naming of an apostolic administrator for the archdiocese.

REVELO: You mean you would remain archbishop in name while another would actually govern? (ROMERO *nods in the affirmative*.) But who would he appoint?

ROMERO: I don't know. He asked me about my "apostolic conversion."

REVELO: Your what?

ROMERO: You know, my supposed "transformation" regarding the poor. I told him I had always taken the problems of the people to heart. He even had a dossier on me. He pointed out my humble origins, my working class parents, my membership in the "conservative" Opus Dei.

REVELO: What's wrong with that? I'm a member of Opus Dei, as is the Pope.

ROMERO: Yes, but I told him that when I was Bishop of Santa María I saw the children dying because of the polluted water they were forced to drink. I told him that Opus Dei never offered to help the children of Santa María.

REVELO: That's unfortunate. What else did the Holy Father say?

ROMERO: He asked me what the saddest part of my life was. I told him the death of Father Grande and all the other priests and lay workers who have fallen.

REVELO: So then, he merely questioned and accused?

ROMERO: He told me to continue to defend social justice and love the poor, but to be careful of ideologies that only replace one type of oppression with another.

REVELO: Well, there you go. You should listen to what he says!

ROMERO: But Revelo, El Salvador isn't communist Poland. I'll be frank with you, I'm thinking of resigning.

REVELO: No, you can't do that.

ROMERO: This is my last chance to get out.

REVELO: No, no, you've got to play this drama through to the end!

ROMERO: Go on, Revelo, go back to the hotel. I have a great deal of thinking and praying to do. (*Exit* REVELO. RO-MERO *kneels at the tomb.*) Saint Peter, blessed Saint Peter, upon whose foundations the first Roman church was built. Guide me through these troubled times!

TEMPTER: (*Voice off.*) Romero. Romero! Romero!

ROMERO: You heed my prayers?

TEMPTER: I hear you.

ROMERO: Blessed Saint Peter—is it really you?

TEMPTER: It is as you wish, my son, what ails you?

ROMERO: The ills of the world.

TEMPTER: (*Appearing before him out of the mist.*) Do you remember the time our Lord was tempted in the wilderness? (*The* TEMPTER *looks like a kindly old man.*)

ROMERO: Yes, I do.

TEMPTER: What did He say after the tempter approached and said, "if you are the Son of God, tell these stones to become bread?"

ROMERO: "Man does not live by bread alone."

TEMPTER: If Jesus had turned stones into bread, mankind would have followed him like a flock of sheep, grateful and obedient.

ROMERO: But what would faith be worth if it was bought by the promise of bread?

TEMPTER: Aren't some of your priests preaching that the only crime is hunger? They write on their banners, "Feed man, and then ask of him virtue."

ROMERO: Yes, they want man to have both spiritual and earthly bread.

TEMPTER: Very good reply, Romero. But I must warn you, there are many cries in the wilderness calling for your head.

ROMERO: I answer only to God.

TEMPTER: They bring many charges against you. (*Enter three* BISHOP *apparitions.*)

ROMERO: Who are they?

TEMPTER: Your tormentors.

BISHOP #1: Your ideas are those of a rebel who shares in the communist takeover of El Salvador. You follow the ideological line of the Third World Liberation movement. You assert that capitalism is perverse and that socialism is Christian.

BISHOP #2: You have totally damaged relations with the state. You insulted the president by not attending his Inauguration. You call the president a liar. You urge the people to oppose the regime, to overthrow it, to replace it with another.

BISHOP #3: You curse the landowners and break off relations with them. You urge the people to resist and liberate the land by force of arms.

TEMPTER: Answer your accusers, Romero! (ROMERO *remains silent.*)

BISHOP #1: You oppose the civilizing actions of the Armed Forces. You taint the army by painting it in the role of repressor and torturer. You call for civil disobedience on the part of the soldiers.

BISHOP #2: You formed so-called "Christian Base Communities" which are really political cadres that spread subversion.

BISHOP #3: You are responsible for the deaths of dozens of priests and layworkers, hundreds of soldiers, and thousands of campesinos.

TEMPTER: Is your silence a sign of guilt? (ROMERO *says nothing. He kneels and prays.*)

BISHOP #1: (*As they all surround* ROMERO, *babbling in tongues.*) You have broken radically with the liturgy by using lay people to celebrate the Eucharist!

BISHOP #2: You have instituted a sacrilegious liturgy of maize among the Indian population!

BISHOP #3: You have allowed the use of coffee and donuts to celebrate the Eucharist!

ROMERO: (*Praying to himself.*) Our Father who art in Heaven, hallowed be Thy name, Thy Kingdom come, Thy will be done on earth as it is in Heaven ...

TEMPTER: Most serious of all is the charge that you carry revolution from within the Church and condemn the Holy See by not carrying out his order to cease Church involvement in temporal affairs!

ROMERO: Hail Mary, full of grace, the Lord is with thee. Blessed art thou among women and blessed is the fruit of thy womb, Jesus.

TEMPTER: You are on the parapet of the temple, Romero, and in danger of falling into the abyss. Throw yourself into your grave, Romero. But there are no angels to break your fall! Your face will crack into a thousand pieces! (*Grabbing* ROMERO *by the hair.*) Do you want to die!

ROMERO: No!

TEMPTER: Are you trying to commit suicide?

ROMERO: No, suicide, never. Never!

TEMPTER: Are you searching for martyrdom!

ROMERO: No, the martyr is chosen by God!

TEMPTER: (*Beginning to take off his mask.*) You conceited little man! I can see right through you! You're using your preaching to promote your candidacy for the Nobel Peace Prize!

ROMERO: (*Rising, trying to move away.*) God help me!

TEMPTER: (*Slowly revealing himself for what he really is.*) You want all the kingdoms of the hereafter revealed to you? Think of it, this crypt in the cathedral, pilgrims paying homage, your enemies in another place!

ROMERO: I won't do the right deed for the wrong reason!

TEMPTER: (*Becoming the devil.*) Saint Romero of the Americas!

ROMERO: Satan, begone!

TEMPTER: You noble bastard!

ROMERO: You shall do homage to the Lord thy God and worship
    him alone!
TEMPTER: (*Producing a chalice and coming towards* ROMERO.)
    I offered you life and you chose death.
ROMERO: May this cup be taken from me!
TEMPTER: Then drink from the bitter chalice! (*Breaking cup on
    floor.*)
ROMERO: Father, Thy will be done!
TEMPTER: Then die! (*The* TEMPTER *and three* BISHOPS *vanish, leaving* ROMERO *collapsed on the floor.*)

*1979—YEAR THREE OF ROMERO'S MINISTRY. "HE HAS
PULLED DOWN PRINCES FROM THEIR THRONES AND EXALTED THE LOWLY"—LUKE 1:52.*

CELESTINA: (*Talking directly to the audience.*) One year it did
    not rain, as if the heavens refused to wash away the blood
    from the streets of the city and the fields of the country.
    Death became a daily occurrence. Corpses began to appear on the streets. At first the people would cover them
    with a blanket and pray for their souls. But after a time
    a headless corpse would appear on the street and people
    would merely turn their heads and pass on. In neighboring Nicaragua, a popular insurgency overthrew the fifty
    year old Somoza dynasty. More and more, the United
    States began to take an interest in what was happening in
    our poor, suffering country. (*Fade on* CELESTINA, *lights
    up on* AMERICAN AMBASSADOR *and* MADAME OLIGARCHY.)
OLIGARCHY: Some of the priests say we are exploiters, but,
    Mr. Ambassador, nothing could be further from the truth.
    Without us there would be no jobs. Our entrepreneurial
    spirit is the country's richest natural resource. Our lands
    were the most productive in the Western World. The
    problem is there is not enough land for all.
AMBASSADOR: Let our land reform exports try and stop the insurgency.
OLIGARCHY: Land reform? We call it "confiscation." It has done
    more to undermine the economy than the reds. After the
    government grabbed our coffee plantations, the country's
    balance of payments suffered.
AMBASSADOR: If the peasants were busy growing their own food,
    they wouldn't join the rebellion.

OLIGARCHY: They need jobs, not land. Our entrepreneurs need more efficient and larger farms like in the States. The small farmer with his two hundred hectares cannot compete in the world market.

AMBASSADOR: We've managed to convince your presidente that land reform is in the best interest.

OLIGARCHY: When Washington barks, he jumps.

AMBASSADOR: He also agreed to rein in his more unscrupulous and corrupt officers.

OLIGARCHY: Did he agree to stop his cronies from sacking the National Treasury?

AMBASSADOR: Look, your aid could be in jeopardy.

OLIGARCHY: Do you want to turn this country over to the communists?

AMBASSADOR: What if the next president were a civilian, freely elected by the people?

OLIGARCHY: Please! Elections have been repeatedly discredited here. They vote for the best propaganda machine, just like in the U.S.

AMBASSADOR: Who do you think should be president?

OLIGARCHY: Someone who can maintain order and promote progress. Major Roberto D'Abussion would make an excellent candidate.

AMBASSADOR: The archbishop's people claim D'Abussion is the leader of the death squads.

OLIGARCHY: The Archbishop! The sacred masses have degenerated into protest meetings. The Catholic radio station mouths the sayings of Radio Habana, Cuba. Romero, once a humble priest, has become a professional agitator. Listen to what he said while he was off in Europe promoting himself for the Nobel Peace Prize. (*Reading.*) "I have warned the oligarchy time and again to open their hands, give away their fancy rings, because if they don't, the time will come when they will be cut off." Now, is that a very Christian thing to say? (*Exit* OLIGARCHY.)

ROMERO: (*At the pulpit.*) Jesus saw a vast crowd and he pitied them, for they were like sheep without a shepherd. Our people, too, give that impression. But like a flock that looks for unity, they find in the Gospel the answer to their problems. God grant that Nicaragua and all the nations of the world find that good Shepherd-King. But "woe to the shepherds who mislead and scatter the flock of my pasture," says the Lord.

AMBASSADOR: (*With* PRESIDENTE.) We are ordering a military alert for the entire Central American region. The cancer in Nicaragua must not be allowed to spread.

PRESIDENTE: That is why you need me now, more than ever. Here we make our stand! (AMBASSADOR *hands* PRESIDENTE *an envelope*.) What's this, more aid?

AMBASSADOR: A one-way ticket to Miami. You could resign as a convincing demonstration of your genuine desire for democracy.

PRESIDENTE: You can't dismiss me like this! I am the duly elected presidente of the republic, guardian of the constitution! (*Fade on* PRESIDENTE *as* AMBASSADOR *descends scaffolding to meet with* ROMERO.)

ROMERO: Jeremiah too condemned the expulsions, the ruling by fear. I saw people living in terror in the villages of Chalatenango. There are men who can't go home, who have to live in the hills like frightened sheep. Let the lessons of Nicaragua be learned in El Salvador. Power cannot be made an absolute, a God. (*Applause*.)

CHORUS: (*Off.*) ¡El Pueblo Unido! ¡Jamás será vencido! (*Repeat.*)

CELESTINA: (*Entering.*) The American Ambassador is here to see you.

ROMERO: Show him in.

AMBASSADOR: Your Excellency, I am very pleased to finally make your acquaintance.

ROMERO: The pleasure is mine, Señor Ambassador.

AMBASSADOR: I want to let you know that we respect your opinion and look forward to working with the Church.

ROMERO: We are glad your great country has taken an interest in our dilemma and hope you will use your considerable influence to further an opening toward dialogue. Otherwise, I forsee civil war.

AMBASSADOR: I agree. I know that we are of one mind in that we loath to see one totalitarian regime replaced by another. You saw what happened to the Church in communist Cuba.

ROMERO: That was most unfortunate.

AMBASSADOR: (*Looking up where the* PRESIDENTE *and* OLIGARCHY *appear in a heated argument*.) You are aware of the coup which is about to take place?

ROMERO: Yes, certain progressive Army officers have consulted with us.

AMBASSADOR: I believe your president is going to resign for, uh, reasons of health. (*Exit* PRESIDENTE, *crestfallen.*) I have been assured that it will be bloodless.

ROMERO: It pleases me that you are for a democratic aperture in El Salvador.

AMBASSADOR: I also want you to know that I personally admire your noble stand on human rights. Is it true that you were nominated for the Nobel Peace Prize by British Parliamentarians? (ROMERO *nods in the affirmative.*) You deserve it. (*Shaking his hand.*) I hope we can work together for the good of the Salvadorean people.

ROMERO: I hope so too. God bless you, Mr. Ambassador. (CELESTINA *shows the* AMBASSADOR *out.*)

CELESTINA: Do you think he is sincere?

ROMERO: I give every man the benefit of the doubt until they prove me wrong.

REVELO: (*Entering.*) Good news! The presidente has flown to Guatemala. The coup is successful! And only one casualty!

ROMERO: Thanks be to God. I hope the junta keeps its promise of reform.

REVELO: You need to go on the radio right away to ask the people for calm. The leftists are calling for a popular insurrection, and outbreaks of violence have already begun.

ROMERO: (*From the pulpit.*) I call on the populace to be patient in looking for change. I ask the privileged to listen to the voice of the poor. I ask the government to remember its reason for being is to serve the people. The Church is ready to cooperate. I must speak out against violence on all sides. The burning of urban transport buses, the machine-gunning of residences, the kidnapping of innocent civilians, and the occupation of offices and churches are wrong. One cannot do evil in order to achieve good.

CAMPESINA: (*Entering.*) Monseñor! Monseñor! Some say that the coup is a trick. They say the right wing is just changing one face for another.

ROMERO: No, the president of the Central American University is on the junta. He even asked me for support before joining. His academic background will act as a check against the military.

CAMPESINA: But you're undermining the popular opposition. The junta hasn't told you they've killed or wounded over one hundred people.

ROMERO: These uprisings are premature and irresponsible. Insurrection is licit only when rational means are exhausted.

CAMPESINA: But we're paying for this "experiment in democracy" with our blood.

REVELO: The security forces must learn to deal with such outbreaks in a less violent way.

CAMPESINA: A less violent way! No, no, Monseñor, we feel cheated.

ROMERO: Why?

CAMPESINA: You did not consult with us before giving your blessing to this new junta.

ROMERO: But Micaela, now we really have the law on our side.

CAMPESINA: The law is like a serpent, it bites those who are barefoot.

ROMERO: Don't say that. Many of the people in the new junta are honest and sincere. Don't you trust me?

CAMPESINA: Yes, Monseñor. But we don't trust them! (*Exit* CAMPESINA.)

CELESTINA: (*To* ROMERO.) Perhaps she's right. Look at these reports. Striking laborers brutally expelled from their factories. The church and rectory of Soyapango searched and the pastor arrested and beaten.

ROMERO: We must give the new junta a chance to prove itself!

REVELO: (*Privately, to* CELESTINA.) Sister, Patience is one of the virtues. I don't know if you realize this, but every day you become more and more like Father Barrera! (*Exit* REVELO *and* CELESTINA. *The set darkens. Enter* CHORUS *with candles.*)

CHORUS: (*Like the choir in a Mass.*) At a place called El Despertar, Father Ortiz Luna and four youths were awakened. At a place called El Despertar, thirty young men who had gathered for a weekend retreat were awakened.

ROMERO: (*From the pulpit.*) The retreat house at El Despertar has been used as a place of evangelical reunions for the last five years. It belongs to the Church and is run by nuns. There is a food cooperative and a medical clinic.

CHORUS: It is not used for subversive meetings. It is not a weapons depot. It is not a guerrilla training center.

ROMERO: At six o'clock in the morning they were awakened by uniformed personnel who broke in firing their arms. An armored car crashed through the steel gates and entered the central patio.

CHORUS: Father Ortiz went to investigate the noises. Father Ortiz fell in the patio outside. Father Ortiz was crushed by an armored car.

ROMERO: Four other young men died of gunshots, two of them only fifteen years old. Soldiers carried the four bodies to the roof of the building, pressed pistols into their hands and photographed them.

CHORUS: The guitars became weapons. The songbooks, subversive literature. The youth, guerrillas.

ROMERO: The police arrested the survivors, even the small children of one of the cooks. Why don't the security forces admit their mistakes? Why do they make it worse by lying? They only lower the credibility of the government.

CHORUS: Why don't they admit their mistakes? Why do they make it worse by lying? Why doesn't the news media print the truth?

ROMERO: Let me say that the Church, like a mother who cannot forget the misery in which her children find themselves, cries for the eternal rest of the victims. But, we also pray for the conversion of the assassins.

CHORUS: Father Ortiz died with his face crushed. In a place called El Despertar, The Awakening. What a horrible awakening!

ROMERO: In order to repair his skull, the mortician had to go to great lengths. Father Ortiz was transformed. He gave his life, his countenance, for Christ. This is what the Lord asks of us, if need be. But I am happy to tell you, fellow Christians, that today, when it is more dangerous than ever to be a priest, we are receiving more vocations in the seminary. This year will break the record—twenty-seven young high school graduates are entering the new seminary class.

CHORUS: The government says there is no persecution of the Church. The government says the infamous fourteen rich families do not exist. The government says there are no disappeared persons.

ROMERO: The night before, a journalist phoned me from Mexico and asked about the government's statements. I told him that the best comment was what had just happened. And I told the journalist: note that the conflict is not between the Church and the government; it is between the government and the people. And the Church is with the people and the people are with the Church, thanks be to God!

(*Fade on* ROMERO. *The action shifts to* CELESTINA *and* REVELO *outside a church.*)

REVELO: (*Pointing off.*) A group of leftists have taken over the Church of El Rosario. They are holding a soldier hostage and demand the release of one of their comrades.

CELESTINA: Let me handle this. Don't call the police.

REVELO: Do you think me so rash? I'm trying to defuse the situation. They say they will kill him if attacked.

CELESTINA: (*Going up to the door of the church.*) Who's in there? Come on out. You have no right to involve the Church in this.

CAMPESINA: (*Voice off.*) We want you to intervene for us.

CELESTINA: Come on out, let's see who you are. (CAMPESINA, *a scarf around her face, a pistol in her hand, steps out.* REVELO *exits quickly.*)

CAMPESINA: Here I am. The others are inside with the hostage.

CELESTINA: Why have you done this?

CAMPESINA: They took our comrade, Francisco, to the barracks. He's been missing for two weeks. We want him back; from now on it's "an eye for an eye."

CELESTINA: Please, please. Hand the soldier over before the police come. I promise Monseñor will do everything in his power to free your friend.

CAMPESINA: No, we want no more promises. At very least we'll have the satisfaction of taking some of those bastards with us.

CELESTINA: Micaela! I know you! Give me the gun, this is not going to work.

CAMPESINA: (*Taking scarf off.* SOLDADO *enters on his knees, bruised and bloody, his hands bound.*) He raped me, this man raped me!

SOLDADO: I'm sorry, I'm sorry, forgive me!

CAMPESINA: (*Holding the pistol to his head.*) I'm going to kill you! Kill you!

CELESTINA: Micaela, have mercy. Remember what Monseñor said, "How evil this system must be to pit the poor campesino in army uniform against the campesino in the fields."

CAMPESINA: His words mean nothing. What has he done for us! We're worse off than ever.

CELESTINA: Don't lose your faith now when you need it more than ever. (*To the* SOLDADO.) Do you realize that, while you were brutalizing people here, other soldiers in another

part of the country were terrorizing and killing your neighbors?

SOLDADO: Yes, yes, forgive me!

CAMPESINA: Where do you get those arguments from, Sister?

CELESTINA: From God, Micaela, from God. Now give me that
gun. (CAMPESINA *gives her the gun.*)

REVELO: (*Entering.*) Here come the police!

MAJOR: (*Machine gun in hand.*) Well, what have we here! (*Blackout.*)

*FROM 1980 TO 1990 MORE THAN $1 MILLION A DAY IN
U.S. AID HAS GONE TO EL SALVADOR, A NATION THE SIZE
OF MASSACHUSETTS, WITH SOME FIVE MILLION PEOPLE.*

AMBASSADOR: (*With* ROMERO *at the chancellery.*) I hear you're
going to send a letter to the President of the United States,
asking him not to send any more military aid to the junta!

ROMERO: Yes, the arms you ship only sharpen the repression
against our defenseless populace.

AMBASSADOR: But the junta needs to maintain order. It'll soon
be phased out and a democratic government installed.
What do you think about Napoleón Duarte? Don't you
think he'll make a good president?

ROMERO: The Christian Democrat? A figurehead. The real power
will remain in the hands of the military. (*Enter a new*
PRESIDENTE *up on the scaffold, a carbon copy of the
old.* MADAME OLIGARCHY *and* BISHOP ÁLVAREZ
stand with him.)

AMBASSADOR: The days of military rule are over. A new order
is rising. Much of the oligarchy has fled, and the new
president is deeply committed to human rights.

PRESIDENTE: I intend to make liberty and justice the corner-
stones of my campaign. (OLIGARCHY *and* ÁLVAREZ
pat him on the back.) Together we can bridge the divi-
sions that separate us and guide El Salvador back to a
new dawn.

ROMERO: Why don't you send us seed and tractors instead of
arms?

PRESIDENTE: First of all, we will solve the security problem by
offering a blanket amnesty to all the rebels. (ÁLVAREZ
and OLIGARCHY *scowl.*) Provided the rebels lay down
their arms first and renounce violence! (*They applaud.*)
We invite our countrymen to join us in the electoral process. Ballots, not bullets!

AMBASSADOR: (*Pointing to the above.*) Isn't this what we want to see?

ROMERO: (*As the scene on high fades away.*) Look, Ambassador, we tried that route. It failed. I am asking your president, in the name of the Christian doctrine he professes, to guarantee that the United States will not intervene to influence the destiny of the Salvadorean people.

AMBASSADOR: Are you prepared to see the leftists take over? Do you want another Cuba, another Nicaragua?

ROMERO: It doesn't have anything to do with communism. It's the legitimate right to self determination that permits the people to set their own historical direction.

AMBASSADOR: There is nothing that will deter you from releasing this letter?

ROMERO: I ask him, I pray you, as leaders of the most democratic country on earth, accept my humble petition!

AMBASSADOR: You went too far this time, Bishop! (*Exit AMBASSADOR.*)

ROMERO: (*A knock is heard.*) Who is it? (ROMERO *opens door, enter* SOLDADO.) What do you want?

SOLDADO: To make a confession.

ROMERO: These are not the right hours.

SOLDADO: Not that kind of confession.

ROMERO: I'm listening.

SOLDADO: They have taken Sister Celestina.

ROMERO: Who!

SOLDADO: The police.

ROMERO: Where?

SOLDADO: The Central Police Station.

ROMERO: Why are you telling me this?

SOLDADO: Because I made a vow to Micaela López. You see, she spared my life.

ROMERO: Where is she?

SOLDADO: I don't know. They took her away to El Playón.

ROMERO: El Playón! Where they find all the dead bodies?

SOLDADO: Yes, there's no hope for her. But there's still time to save Sister Celestina.

ROMERO: Yes, of course, thank you, my son. May God bless you. (*They both exit.*)

REVELO: (*With the* MAJOR *at the Police Station.*) I want to understand something perfectly clear. You say you've been assigned to Monseñor's security detail?

MAJOR: Exactly.

REVELO: And because of his stubborn refusal to accept any security for his person you are doing this incognito?

MAJOR: Precisely.

REVELO: You want to know his daily schedule so that you many
provide adequate protection for him?

MAJOR: Of course.

REVELO: We are all aware of those vicious rumors directed toward
his person. For he has made some very powerful people
quite furious.

MAJOR: He has.

REVELO: Forces, dark forces, seek his annihilation.

MAJOR: He must be protected in spite of himself.

REVELO: You will see that no harm comes to him?

MAJOR: We'll provide around the clock protection.

REVELO: That's what he needs. (*Handing over some papers.*)
Well, I must be off. Good night, Major.

MAJOR: Wait.

REVELO: What?

MAJOR: Anything else?

REVELO: Like what?

MAJOR: Don't you want anything?

REVELO: Like what!

MAJOR: Some modest compensation?   (*Moving towards* RE-
VELO.)

REVELO: No! No thank you!

MAJOR: In keeping with tradition! Please take it, I insist! (*Pressing money into* REVELO*'s hand.*)

REVELO: No, no, I don't want it! I don't want anything to do
with it! (*They exit.*)

REPORTER: (*With* AMBASSADOR *at his office.*) My sources report that an assassination attempt will be made on Romero's life within the next twenty-four hours.

AMBASSADOR: So tell me, Kathy, how were you privy to this
information?

REPORTER: I got it straight from the horse's mouth, Bill.

AMBASSADOR: I'll contact him right away. (*Exit* REPORTER.
AMBASSADOR *dials phone and* ROMERO *picks it up on
the other end.*)

ROMERO: Hello? Yes, Ambassador. Extra precautions? I have no
bodyguards, other than my unarmed parishioners. Why?
Well, they have no bodyguards.

AMBASSADOR: You don't seem to understand the seriousness of this. If something should happen to you, my government ...

ROMERO: Would be embarrassed?

AMBASSADOR: Why do you say that?

ROMERO: Because you are the Romans!

AMBASSADOR: (*Face to face with* ROMERO *now.*) Why don't you leave the country for a while? Take a vacation. We'll pay for it!

ROMERO: No thank you, I can't afford to take vacations.

AMBASSADOR: But your life is in grave danger.

ROMERO: Ambassador, I do appreciate your concern, but I am the pastor of my sheep ...

AMBASSADOR: Don't speak in parables to me!

ROMERO: It's true. I'm a simple country priest who trusts in the way of the Lord. My life is in His hands.

AMBASSADOR: Reconsider my offer for exile. What good will you be to the people dead!

ROMERO: Exile is it! I see. But even if your sources are correct, I still can't leave.

AMBASSADOR: You want to die!

ROMERO: No. But as a Christian, I don't believe in death without resurrection. If they kill me, I will rise again in the Salvadorean people. I am not boasting or saying this out of pride, but rather as humbly as I can.

AMBASSADOR: Oh, wait a minute! What role are you trying to cast me in!

ROMERO: As a shepherd, I am obliged by divine law to give my life for those I love, including my would-be assassins. And if they should go so far as to carry out their threats, I want you to know that I now offer my blood to God for the resurrection of El Salvador.

AMBASSADOR: You think you're the Savior, don't you? Well, history doesn't repeat itself.

ROMERO: You and I have a different interpretation of history.

AMBASSADOR: Don't be a martyr, Romero! Martyrs don't exist anymore. You're an anachronism!

ROMERO: I told you, I'm not looking for martyrdom. That is a grace of God I am not worthy of. But, if God wants me as a sacrifice, then I only hope that my blood will be like a seed.

AMBASSADOR: Well then, damn you! Go! Go! Do what your destiny calls for!

ROMERO: The bishop may die, but the Church of God, which is the people, will never perish.

AMBASSADOR: I warned you! I did everything in my power to dissuade you. Don't blame me! (*Exit* AMBASSADOR.)

CELESTINA: (*Entering as* AMBASSADOR *leaves.*) What's all that shouting? What's the matter with him?

ROMERO: He's just a sore loser.

CELESTINA: You look tired.

ROMERO: It's been a long, dark night.

CELESTINA: Any word about Micaela López?

ROMERO: Don't you worry about her, Celestina, she'll turn up.

CELESTINA: Dead! Don't patronize me, Monseñor. I'm not a little girl.

ROMERO: I'm sorry. But until we find her, dead or alive, I honestly don't know where she is. Although I suspect the worst.

CELESTINA: (*Trying to cheer him up.*) Bishop Álvarez asked me if I had witnessed any change in you these past three years. You used to be so cold, timid, shaking hands like a wet fish. The rumors were that you once had a nervous breakdown.

ROMERO: Oh I've had several! At least once a week! One must be crazy to have this job!

CELESTINA: See, you laugh, make jokes. You've become open and warm. I told the bishop you learned to grow, to change, even to undergo conversion. You see, you adopted a new theology, much to the surprise and alarm of those who preferred the old.

ROMERO: So that was my apostolic conversion.

CELESTINA: Yes, because of your faith in the God of Change you often have to journey alone, misunderstood by many. Like Abraham, you must travel a road with trust in the Spirit of God. "Leave your country, your family and your father's house for the land I will show you."

ROMERO: I really changed that much?

CELESTINA: Yes, by a new and different sense of what it means to be a Christian. And that, in turn, has affected everyone else around you.

ROMERO: The God of Change! I like that. Thanks for cheering me up, Sister. Look, it's almost morning! Let's go have a hearty breakfast! Did they mistreat you at the police station?

CELESTINA: No, but I heard what they do to the women there. One of the guards confessed to me. He wanted to get it off his chest. He told me how they gang-rape the women—in shifts—day and night.

ROMERO: Dios mío.

CELESTINA: The guard told me. "Be careful, Sister, El Salvador is becoming a place where they rape and murder nuns!" (*Exit* ROMERO *and* CELESTINA.)

IN DECEMBER, 1980 FOUR AMERICAN CHURCH-WOMEN: ITA FORD, MAURA CLARKE, DORTHY KAZEL AND JEAN DONOVAN WERE RAPED AND KILLED BY SALVADO-RAN SECURITY FORCES.

MAJOR: (*Entering with his death squad in the persons of* ÁL-VAREZ, OLIGARCHY *and* PRESIDENTE *to perform a grotesque parody of the last supper.*) We now make ready for our last supper!

DEATH SQUAD: (*In unison.*) Last supper!

MAJOR: I will set you an example.

DEATH SQUAD: An example!

MAJOR: We draw lots for the honor of killing him!

DEATH SQUAD: Killing him! (*They draw lots.*)

ROMERO: (*Ascending the pulpit.*) Brothers and sisters, I want to make a special appeal to the soldiers, national guardsmen and policemen. Brothers, each one of you is one of us. We are the same people. The campesinos you kill are your own brothers and sisters! (*Applause.*)

MAJOR: (*Holding a cup aloft.*) Take this cup of blood and drink of it, for it is his blood!

DEATH SQUAD: (*Drinking.*) His blood!

MAJOR: (*Holding up a piece of raw meat.*) Take this meat and eat of it, for it is his body!

DEATH SQUAD: His body!

ROMERO: When you hear the words of a man telling you to kill, remember instead the words of God—"Thou shalt not kill." No soldier is obliged to obey an order contrary to the law of God. It is time that you come to your senses and obey your conscience rather than carry out a sinful command. (*As the* DEATH SQUAD *approaches* ROMERO.) In the name of God, in the name of the tormented people who have suffered so much and whose cries reach out to heaven, I beseech you, I beg you, I order you

in the name of God—stop the repression. Stop the repression! Stop the repression!!

MAJOR: (*Shooting* ROMERO.) Traitor!

ROMERO: (*Clutching his breast.*) Father!

PRESIDENTE: (*Shooting* ROMERO.) Rabble rouser!

ROMERO: (*Falling to his knees.*) Into thy hands ...

OLIGARCHY: (*Shooting* ROMERO.) Communist!

ROMERO: I commit ...

BISHOP: (*Shooting* ROMERO.) Heretic!

ROMERO: My spirit! (ROMERO *dies. Lights dim very low. Exit*
DEATH SQUAD. ROMERO *has also disappeared.*)

CELESTINA: That's how it happened. If you had to do it again,
would you chose the same path?

ROMERO: (*Voice taped.*) Yes! What are those noises?

CELESTINA: The people come to bury you. (*Noises of a large
multitude. The doors of the church swing open allowing
the sunlight to enter.*)

*PHARISEES AND ROMANS—BE GONE! MONSEÑOR,
YOU LIVE ON IN THE SALVADOREAN PEOPLE!*

CELESTINA: (*At the pulpit, priests standing beside her.*) The brief
ministry of Bishop Romero in the Archdiocese of San Salvador had the same characteristics as the ministry of his
Master and Lord in the land of Judea. Monseñor was a
follower of the Jesus who preached words of hope and
tirelessly denounced injustice. Our bishop was accused
of being a blasphemer, a disrupter of public order, and
was assassinated by those who hate the truth. In a sense,
Bishop Romero is not dead. He planted so much love
in such good earth, that the seed will yield a hundred-
fold. The Salvadoran people know that he still lives, and
that the clergy follow in his path and commit themselves
to making sure that his voice will not be silenced. God
will watch over us and see to it that his martyrdom will
bear magnificent fruit. As we bury Bishop Romero and so
many others who have been murdered, we want to repeat
our condemnation of and our protest against this insan-
ity. We are pleading, as he did in his last sermon, for an
end to repression everywhere—on the entire continent,
and especially in this beloved and tormented country of
El Salvador! (*Cheers and applause.*)

PRESIDENTE: (*Entering with other members of the death squad.*)
    He was a dangerous man—leading us to civil war! (*A pike
    in his hand.*)

OLIGARCHY: (*A lash in her hand.*) He didn't care about you—he
    was doing it for his own self-aggrandizement.

REVELO: (*A noose around his neck.*) We were just instruments of
    his divine will.

AMBASSADOR: (*Washing his hands.*) The murder was the work
    of an expert—it could have been the extreme right or the
    extreme left.

MAJOR: (*Holding a crown of thorns.*) The crown of thorns—the
    lashing and humiliation—the crucifixion! Isn't that what
    you all wanted! (*Enter* ROMERO, *very much alive, from
    the audience. The people gather around him, the* DEATH
    SQUAD *exits.*)

CAMPESINA. ¡Oscar Romero, Revolucionario!

PRIEST: ¡Oscar Romero, Pastor!

SOLDADO: ¡Oscar Romero, Martir!

CELESTINA: ¡Oscar Romero, Santo!

ALL: ¡Oscar Romero, presente! ¡Romero! ¡Presente! ¡Presente!
    ¡Presente!

THE END

The Miser of Mexico

(Freely stolen from Moliere who borrowed it from Plautus)

CHARACTERS

DON PROFUNDO QUEQUEMÁFER, a miser.
CLEMENTE, his son.
ELISA, his daughter.
VALENTÍN DE LA SIERRA, in love with Elisa.
MARIANA, fair maid in love with Clemente.
FILERO, servant of Clemente.
TAN-TAN, valet, cook, coachman, waiter, butler, etc. to Don Profundo.
FANNY, Mariana's aunt.
MARUJA, the maid.
GENERALÍSIMO RABIOSO RESBALOSO, a wealthy crony of Don Profundo.
PANCHO PÉREZ, a Revolutionary.

TIME AND PLACE

1910, the eve of the Mexican Revolution. Northern Mexico.

ACT ONE

Morning. The outdoor patio in the casa grande of DON PRO-
FUNDO QUEQUEMÁFER. *Enter two servants,* FILERO *and* MA-
RUJA, *in a passionate argument.*

FILERO: (*Keeping pace with* MARUJA, *who is sweeping the floor.*)
¡Maruja, querida! Please, come with me! (*Trying to hug
her.*)

MARUJA: (*Shrugging him off.*) No, I'm not going anywhere with
you. All you are is a bag of hot air.

FILERO: But, mi amor, if we can just get to el otro lado ... (*Trying
to embrace her.*)

MARUJA: Why should I want to go to "the other side" with the
North Americanos? They don't even speak Spanish!

FILERO: But, mi amor, there are plenty of jobs we can work at in
the United Estates.

MARUJA: No, gracias. I'll just stay here en mi tierra. Maybe I'll
marry Tan-Tan! Or Fidencio, the butcher. At least I have
plenty of meat to eat!

FILERO: Oh, mi amor, don't say these things, you break my corazón! (*Getting down on his knees.*) I would do anything
for you—lie, steal, murder ...

MARUJA: I don't believe you! You men are all alike!

FILERO: Mira, I'll prove it to you. Here's the wedding ring! (*Takes
a very modest little ring out of his pocket, shines it on his
zarape, and shows it to her.*)

MARUJA: Oh, how nice! Isn't that the same ring you gave to
Juanita that she threw back in your face? What am I, the
second guitarra!

FILERO: (*Placing the ring in her hand and kissing it.*) No, mi amor,
you are the salsa in my taquitos. (MARUJA *beams.*) The
guacamole in my salad!

MARUJA: Oh, a poet! (*Puts the ring on her finger and admires it.*)

FILERO: The sour cream in my enchiladas!

MARUJA: Oh stop! Say no more! (*Taking her ring and starting to
exit.*) I'll think about it.

FILERO: How about a little besito? (*Puckering his lips for a kiss.*)

MARUJA: (*Going to kiss him.* MARUJA *sees* ELISA *coming.*)
No, no, no, no, no. Vete, vete, go! Here comes the little

mistress. (MARUJA *and* FILERO *exit from opposite ends of the stage.*)

ELISA: (*Enters with* VALENTÍN. *They are also having a lovers' quarrel.*) I told you, I can't see you anymore, it is all over between us.

VALENTÍN: Elisa, querida, why are you so angry?

ELISA: I am not angry. But this situation is impossible! People suspect us. My father would never approve of my seeing a servant in his household.

VALENTÍN: There's only one thing to do then—we must elope!

ELISA: Impossible, Valentín. Don't you see, we are of different classes. The world would censure us.

VALENTÍN: Elisa, I never thought you would let that come between us.

ELISA: Oh, Valentín, if only others saw you as I do. Every day I think about how you risked your life to save mine from Apache Indians in the burning deserts of Chihuahua and escorted us safely here to Ciudad Juárez.

VALENTÍN: Yes, Elisa, and I fell in love with you the moment I saw you. That is why I accepted your Father's so called "reward" to stay on this rancho and act as his mayordomo.

ELISA: I know that if my father only knew how noble your spirit is, he would bank on that as currency for my hand.

VALENTÍN: Elisa, I pray you, tell me the cause of your affliction, so that I may rub the blemish out!

ELISA: Oh, I am so confused! My father has been saying things to me!

VALENTÍN: What did he say?

ELISA: He says that a fair-skinned girl like me can expect to marry a wealthy man of European blood!

VALENTÍN: So, that's it! His avarice and high-tone airs cause him to look down on me! And he's gone and poisoned your mind! Then, there's nothing left for me here. I might as well go and join my brother Pancho ...

ELISA: The revolucionario?

VALENTÍN: Yes, with the Resistance, in the mountains.

ELISA: Oh!

VALENTÍN: Adiós, Elisa. (*Turning as though to leave.*)

ELISA: Valentín, don't go! Let us think of some way of winning my father's approval.

VALENTÍN You don't disdain me for the color of my skin?

ELISA: Chocolate is my favorite drink.

VALENTÍN: And I am very fond of vanilla. (*They embrace.*) Oh, Elisa, why is it that your father only loves power and money.

ELISA: There's nothing wrong with being comfortable, Valentín. After all, man does not live by bread alone!

VALENTÍN: If I was a rich landowner, or an important bureaucrat, he would hand you over in the wink of eye. (*Sees* CLEMENTE *coming.*) Look, here comes your brother.

ELISA: Get him to help us.

VALENTÍN: But he's *your* brother. Why don't you try to gain his confidence?

ELISA: I don't know if I have the courage to confide in him. Tell him about your noble cause.

VALENTÍN: You don't think he would betray us?

ELISA: Oh, you don't know him. He's a very idealistic person with high principles, just the opposite of my father.

VALENTÍN: (*AS* CLEMENTE *enters.*) Good morning, Clemente.

CLEMENTE: Hello, Valentín. Elisa, Elisa, you won't believe what has happened to me. I'm bursting over with joy.

VALENTÍN: Perhaps I should take my leave.

CLEMENTE: No, no, stay. I want the whole world to know that I am in love!

ELISA: You're in love, querido hermano!

CLEMENTE: Yes, love! Have you ever been in love? (*He interrupts her before she has a chance to speak.*) Of course not, how could you! Well, I am.

ELISA: And, who is this girl?

CLEMENTE: Ah, that's another problem. But don't try to dissuade me, dear sister. You don't understand the way Cupid's arrows pierce our very soul.

ELISA: I might surprise you in that.

CLEMENTE: The one who has stolen my heart is—Mariana!

ELISA *and* VALENTÍN: The servant girl!

VALENTÍN: Why, dear Clemente, how could you possibly marry beneath your rank and station?

CLEMENTE: Valentín, it is unfortunate that we live in a world where class is a measure of one's worth. We should judge people by their good deeds, not by their good clothes. (*As he brushes off some lint on his expensive jacket.*) Besides, Mariana is not a servant. My father "adopted" her after he coldly and callously foreclosed on her mother's estate.

ELISA: Oh, Clemente, what a cruel world is this!

CLEMENTE: And so, Elisa, I don't care that my peers will look at me askance, or that she will not be accepted into polite society. I will suffer the slings and arrows of disdain along with her.

VALENTÍN: We know exactly what you're going through, Clemente.

CLEMENTE: How could you? Don't you see that my father will never approve of this match?

ELISA: Oh, but that's exactly what I wanted to talk to you about, dear brother.

CLEMENTE: Have you ever seen anything more cruel than this tightfisted budget exercised over us? What good will wealth do us, if it comes when we are no longer young enough to enjoy it?

VALENTÍN: Clemente, we have a confession to make.

CLEMENTE: Oh, let me guess. (*Beat.*) You two are in love!

ELISA: Why brother, how did you know that!

CLEMENTE: Well, it's fairly obvious. All those deep sighs, knowing glances, husky whispers. That's why I decided to tell you about my own affair! I hope you'll both be very happy. You have my blessings.

VALENTÍN: (*Embracing* CLEMENTE.) Thank you, Clemente, for your approval. I assure you that I have nothing but the best intentions towards Elisa.

CLEMENTE: I knew it all along. You're a good fellow, Valentín.

VALENTÍN: Now there's something I want to tell you. What do you think about the current "troubles"?

CLEMENTE: It's a sad state of affairs.

VALENTÍN: Would you say that the common people are fed up with their rulers?

CLEMENTE: Absolutely, and they have every right to be.

VALENTÍN: Would you say that a dramatic insurrection is about to engulf Mexico?

CLEMENTE: Any day now—the old guard is on its way out!

VALENTÍN: Then you believe in the principles of the Revolution!

CLEMENTE: Oh, please, Valentín, don't talk to me of revolution. The common people are incapable of grasping even the simplest concepts of self-government. And who's going to lead them ... the bandidos?

VALENTÍN: They are not bandidos, they are revolutionaries!

CLEMENTE: You're confusing rebels with ruffians!

ELISA: Come, come, come. Argue somewhere else! I think I hear my father coming. (*Exit* CLEMENTE, VALENTÍN,

ELISA.)

DON: (*Entering with* FILERO.) Don't you dare talk back to me. Get out of my house! ¡Pelado! ¡Estafador!

FILERO: (*Aside.*) I've never seen anyone so wicked as this accursed old zopilote!

DON: What are you muttering about?

FILERO: My master, your son, gave me orders to wait for him.

DON: Wait for him out in the street. I won't have someone hovering around me, coveting everything, and sneaking about to see if there's anything he can rob.

FILERO: How can a man be robbed who locks up everything and stands guard day and night?

DON: I lock things up and stand guard to keep thieves like you at bay. (*Aside.*) Doesn't he look like a bandido? I'm afraid he suspects where my money is. (*To* FILERO.) Are you one of those who goes around spreading rumors that people like me have bank notes hidden in the house?

FILERO: You have bank notes hidden in the house?

DON: No, you villain, I didn't say that! (*Aside.*) I'm sure he's one of those insurrectionists who goes around robbing decent people of their hard earned money. (*To* FILERO.) Get out of my house!

FILERO: But your son, my master ...

DON: Argue, will you! (*Raising his hand to give* FILERO *a box on the ear.*) I'll beat you within an inch of your life!

FILERO: All right, I'm going.

DON: Wait! Are you taking anything of mine?

FILERO: What could I have of yours?

DON: Come here. Let's see. Have you stolen any huevos from my chickens?

FILERO: No.

DON: Let's see them.

FILERO: What?

DON: The huevos.

FILERO: Which ones?

DON: (*Pointing at his zarape.*) Those.

FILERO: (*Grabbing the area of his groin.*) Oh no, not these!

DON: Have you put anything in there? (*Motioning* FILERO *up on a bench.*) Get up there! These blasted zarapes are just right for hiding stolen goods, and I wish people could be hanged for wearing them. (*Looking under* FILERO's *zarape.*)

FILERO: (*Aside.*) Oh, how I'd like to make his fears come true! What joy I'd have in robbing him!

DON: (*Hearing "robbing."*) Eh? What did you say about robbing?

FILERO: I said that you poke about everywhere to see if I'm robbing you.

DON: (*Going around back to feel* FILERO's *pockets.*) That's exactly what I intend to do.

FILERO: Oh, a plague upon avaricious old men!

DON: What's that? What did you say?

FILERO: I said, "a plague on avarice."

DON: Avarice?

FILERO: Yes, one of the deadly sins. The priest talked about it in church last Sunday.

DON: The priest! (*Aside.*) Is that blasted priest trying to stir up trouble? (*To* FILERO.) What else did the priest say about these avaricious men.

FILERO: He said they're scoundrels, skinflints and bloodsuckers.

DON: Did the priest name any names?

FILERO: No, everybody knows who they are. And they'll be punished come judgement day. (DON PROFUNDO *makes a face.*) What are you so upset about?

DON: I'm upset about what I should be upset about. Were you speaking about me?

FILERO: No, I was speaking to ... to my sombrero!

DON: I may knock your sombrero right off your head.

FILERO: Nobody mentioned your name.

DON: If you talk any more, I may have to give you a cowhiding.

FILERO: If the sombrero fits, wear it.

DON: Hold your tongue! Now, give it back to me without all this searching.

FILERO: What?

DON: What you've taken from me.

FILERO: I've taken nothing.

DON: Are you sure?

FILERO: Yes!

DON: Fine. Then the devil take you!

FILERO: There's a fine Christian send-off!

DON: (*Pushing* FILERO *out the door.*) And may you burn in hell! (*Aside.*) That sinverguenza. It's awful having to keep large sums of small change in the house. I've got so much money I don't know what to do with it! God, I hope I did the right thing—hiding the ten thousand pesos I was paid yesterday in my strong box under the floor of

my office. Ten thousand crisp green pesos is a very large
sum of change to have in one's casa. (CLEMENTE *and*
ELISA, *speaking in whispers, appear at the entrance to the
patio.*) Oh heavens! I have given myself away! What are
you doing?

CLEMENTE: Nothing, father.

DON: How long have you been spying on me?

ELISA: Father, we haven't done anything of the sort.

DON: You heard ...

CLEMENTE: What?

DON: What I just said.

ELISA: What did you just say?

DON: Nothing. I merely said how happy a man must be who has
ten thousand crisp new pesos.

ELISA: Hmmmm.

DON: Of course, I wouldn't want you to think it is I who have ten
thousand luscious pesos.

CLEMENTE: Oh no.

DON: Because then I wouldn't complain, as I do now, that times
are hard.

CLEMENTE: Oh, father, everyone knows you're one of the richest
men in Mexico.

DON: What! Whoever says that is a liar and a villain!

ELISA: Please don't get angry.

DON: To think that my own children are spreading such vicious
rumors.

CLEMENTE: Father, we've done no such thing!

DON: And the expenses you run up! We're going bankrupt!

CLEMENTE: What expenses?

DON: Look at the sumptuous apparel you parade around the city
in. You suit yourself in the style of a tycoon. To go about
dressed the way you are, you must certainly be robbing
me.

CLEMENTE: Me robbing you! Father, you know that's not true.

DON: Your ostentatious displays of opulence will cause someone
to come here and cut my throat.

CLEMENTE: Perhaps if you were a bit more generous with your
money, people wouldn't covet it.

DON: What do you expect me to do, hijo, pass it out for free on
the street? Let people work for it like I did, like your
grandfather did, and his father before him!

CLEMENTE: But Father, you didn't have to work. You inherited
your money, like your father and his father before him.

DON: You young rapscallion! Don't you have any respect! Can't you see how I've scraped my fingers to the bone to hold on to what little we have left of our once sizable fortune?

ELISA: (*Humoring* DON PROFUNDO.) That's right, Papi, you have. And some day you'll leave it all to us, verdad?

DON: Provided you both behave and do exactly as I tell you. Now then, I have other important matters to discuss. Eh? (*Seeing* CLEMENTE *and* ELISA *signaling each other in a low voice. Aside.*) I think they're signaling each other to steal my purse. (*Louder.*) What do these signs mean?

ELISA: Clemente and I are debating who should speak first, since we both have something to say to you.

DON: I also have something to say to you.

CLEMENTE: The subject we wish to discuss is marriage.

DON: The subject I wish to discuss is marriage.

ELISA: Ah, Father!

DON: Why daughter, what are you afraid of?

ELISA: I am afraid of marriage the way you think of it, dear Father.

DON: But why? I know what's best for you. But let us begin at the beginning. What do you think of our new maid, Mariana?

CLEMENTE: She is not a maid!

DON: What did you say?

CLEMENTE: She is a fair maid.

DON: Her looks?

CLEMENTE: Angelic.

DON: Very European—unlike some of these indios around here. What about her air and manner?

CLEMENTE: Honest, intelligent, admirable.

DON: I even found that she is of noble blood—partly. On her mother's stepsister's side she is a cousin twice removed of Hernán Cortés' sergeant-at-arms!

CLEMENTE: (*Sarcastically.*) I'm impressed.

DON: Don't you think that a girl like that deserves to be lifted up from her lowly condition?

CLEMENTE: Of course.

DON: Don't you think she would make an excellent housewife?

CLEMENTE: Exceedingly so!

DON: Thus, any man would be quite satisfied with her?

CLEMENTE: Blessed!

DON: Of course, the only drawback is—she has no money.

CLEMENTE: Money should not be a consideration.

DON: Well, I'm so glad you agree with me, Clemente, because I am resolved to marry her.

CLEMENTE: What!

DON: Oh, don't worry, she'll still wait on us hand and foot. That's what wives are for.

CLEMENTE: Wait! What! You are resolved ...

DON: To marry Mariana.

CLEMENTE: Who? You! You?

DON: Yes, I, I. What's got into you, hijo?

CLEMENTE: I suddenly feel very ill. I better go. (*Exit* CLE-MENTE. *Gagging and holding on to his heart.*)

DON: Go to the kitchen immediately and drink a large glass of plain water. (*To* ELISA.) These supercilious sophisticates have no more strength than a wet noodle. Well, so much for one marriage. For your brother, I have in mind a certain widow someone mentioned to me last week. And as for you, I am giving you to El Generalísimo Resbaloso!

ELISA: Rabioso Resbaloso?

DON: Yes! A rich man and a much decorated veteran of the war against the French.

ELISA: That old goat who smells of brandy and stale cigars!

DON: He has excellent taste in tobacco and wine.

ELISA: The man with the wooden leg!

DON: That member was lost on Cinco de Mayo in glorious defense of the Fatherland at Puebla!

ELISA: But he already has a wife!

DON: Alas, the poor lady died last year of rheumatism.

ELISA: But his children are older than I!

DON: At least they're out of the house and not underfoot.

ELISA: Absolutely not!

DON: You'll do as I command!

ELISA: You cannot force me.

DON: I will force you.

ELISA: I will kill myself!

DON: You will do no such thing! Do you know how expensive funerals are these days?

ELISA: How can you marry off your daughter like that?

DON: It's a match made in heaven! And I'll wager that everyone will approve of it.

ELISA: It's a match made in hell and I'll wager everyone will think you've gone mad.

DON: (*Seeing* VALENTÍN *approach.*) Here is Valentín. Are you willing to let him judge us in this matter?

ELISA: Yes! I will abide by his decision.

DON: Here, here. Valentín. We have elected you to decide who is in the right, my daughter or I.

VALENTÍN: You sir, without a doubt.

DON: You heard what we were talking about?

VALENTÍN: No, but you couldn't be wrong. Your name is Profundo, thus you must be profoundly correct.

DON: I wish to give my daughter a husband as rich as he is brave, and she disdains him. What do you say to that?

VALENTÍN: Ahhh. I say that, eh, basically I think you are right. But she might tell you that you are rushing things a bit.

DON: But we can't let this opportunity slip through our fingers, for Don Rabioso promises to take her ...

VALENTÍN: (*Interrupting him.*) RRRRabioso RRResbaloso, the Comandante of the Rural Guards?

DON: Yes, RRRabioso RRResbaloso, the most patriotic soldier in all of Mexico promises to take my daughter ... without a dowry!

VALENTÍN: Ah! Then I will say no more. (*To* ELISA.) Don't you see? This is profound reason! One must submit to it.

ELISA: (*Aside to* VALENTÍN) What! Are you mad!

DON: For me it means a considerable saving.

VALENTÍN: Yes, but others might say that the differences in their ages would surely subject the marriage to unnecessary strain.

DON: But he has influential friends in high places.

VALENTÍN: True, but don't you think some fathers would think more of their daughter's happiness than of the prestige and influence?

DON: But he's the president of the Bank of Chihuahua.

VALENTÍN: Also true, but your daughter might feel uncomfortable living with a man who executes people for a living and that a union which lasts until "death," excuse the pun, ought to be carefully considered.

DON: But he is a war hero.

VALENTÍN: True again, but some people might say that she might resent sharing her body and soul with a man who tortures people on a regular basis.

DON: But he's promised to take her without a dowry!

VALENTÍN: That settles it—without a dowry—how can one resist logic like that?

DON: (*Hearing a sound coming from his office.*) What was that? Is someone opening the door to my office? (*Aside.*) Are they

trying to steal my money? (*To* VALENTÍN *and* ELISA.)
    I'll be right back. (*He exits.*)
ELISA: What the devil are you trying to do?
VALENTÍN: Forgive me, I don't want to anger him, for then we
    shall better achieve our goals. Pretend to consent to his
    wishes until we find some expedient way to break off the
    marriage.
ELISA: And if we don't?
VALENTÍN: I don't know, we'll think of something. Pretend you're
    ill.
ELISA: ¡Dios mío! I fear I'll end up dead like Juliet!
VALENTÍN: Don't say that! Our last resort would be to flee to-
    gether into the mountains and join the Revolution.
ELISA: I don't want to join the Revolution. I just want to live in
    peace here in our little Rancho Grande!
DON: (*Entering.*) False alarm.
VALENTÍN: (*Aloud so* DON PROFUNDO *will hear.*) Yes, a girl
    ought to obey her father.
DON: Well said.
VALENTÍN: Forgive me if I have been too forward in speaking to
    her this way.
DON: Why, no, I think you should assume absolute control over
    her.
VALENTÍN: (*To* ELISA.) Hear that! (*To* DON.) I'll keep a tight
    rein on her.
DON: Good. I'm going for a stroll through town.
VALENTÍN: Yes, Elisa, wealth and power are more precious than
    youth, honor, wisdom, or God! You ought to thank Him
    for the honest father he has given you. When a decent,
    moral Christian soldier promises to take a daughter with-
    out a dowry ... (*Exit* VALENTÍN *and* ELISA.)
DON: Ah. What a fine fellow. Spoken like an oracle. Happy the
    man who has such a servant. (*Exit* DON.)
MARUJA: (*Entering with* FILERO, *gazing at her ring.*) Suppose
    we get married. Tell me, what happens after the wedding?
FILERO: Since you don't want to go to the United States, where
    the streets are paved with gold ... I'll lay claim to a little
    piece of land up there in the sierra ... build a little adobe
    casa ... and get some cows, chickens, pigs and a mule.
    I'll work the fields, you care for the children.
MARUJA: Children? Already you are planning children? You
    want me to go from being a slave to Don Profundo to
    being a slave to you.

FILERO: But, Maruja, querida, this will be our little ranchito. Something that we can sink our teeth into.

MARUJA: Sink our teeth into—a few beans and tortillas! You know what life is like in the sierra—working from sun up to sun down. At least here I get scraps from the table. Paint me another picture, a prettier one, in the city!

FILERO: (*Wringing his zarape.*) Bueno. We move to a big city, Mexico City! I know a little about, uh ... (*Looking at his zarape.*) Zarapes! We'll sell zarapes. You weave them, I'll sell them! In no time, we'll be rich!

MARUJA: Oh, fantástico! I go from being a slave in the Casa Grande of Don Profundo to being a slave in your zarape factory.

FILERO: Maruja! What do you want? We are simple people.

MARUJA: No, you are simple people. I am a smart people. I want more out of life than carrying this broom around. I want no living in the sierra, no zarape factory, no bawling babies bouncing out of my belly year after year!

FILERO: But, Maruja, we got no dinero!

MARUJA: Well, find a way to get some dinero!

FILERO: We can't expect to become millionarios over night! (*Suddenly struck by a thought.*) Wait a minute! Why not! (*Embracing her.*)

MARUJA: Why not what? (*Enter CLEMENTE.*) ¡Quítate! ¡Quítate! ¡Ahí viene el señorito! (CLEMENTE *and* VALENTÍN *enter,* MARUJA *gets all flustered. She pretends to be sweeping, and exits.* FILERO *stands at attention, waiting for his master to finish conversing with* VALENTÍN.)

CLEMENTE: You see, Valentín, things are more pressing than ever. I have discovered that my father is my rival in love.

VALENTÍN: Your father in love!

CLEMENTE: Yes, and I had a hell of a time hiding from him how much this news pained me.

VALENTÍN: Mixing himself up with love! Is he making a mockery of the word? Was love made for someone like him?

CLEMENTE: He leaves me nothing, will probably outlive me, and trys to take that which I love the most. I am resolved to fight back!

VALENTÍN: Then, join us, Clemente!

CLEMENTE: I was thinking, how could I best serve your cause?

VALENTÍN: By getting the key to the powder house and helping us distribute the arms.

CLEMENTE: No, no, no! Let me write a manifesto!

VALENTÍN: A manifesto?

CLEMENTE: Yes, the Manifesto of the Revolution. I'm a wonderful writer, my essays have been published all over the Republic!

VALENTÍN: But Clemente, most of our people can't read! There's no time, publishing is expensive.

CLEMENTE: Not to worry, I'm going to borrow the money. Ah, there's Filero, just the person I need to speak to. Don't worry Valentín, I'll dash off that manifesto and have it for you in no time!

VALENTÍN: Just don't spend too much time on this, Clemente. The Revolution may pass you by! (*Exit* VALENTÍN.)

CLEMENTE: (*Admonishing* FILERO.) Manioso—¡Ya te conozco, mosco! Where have you been?

FILERO: Señor, your father, the codoest hombre in all of Mexico, chased me out of your house.

CLEMENTE: Ni modo—what answer did the lender give you? Do I get my loan or not? I need that money more than ever now!

FILERO: El Generalísimo Resbaloso promised to bring the gentlemen here today.

CLEMENTE: Resbaloso? He's got his nose in this business? Will I get the fifteen thousand pesos I asked for?

FILERO: Yes, but with certain little conditions attached, although the lender proposes to charge no more than twenty-five percent interest.

CLEMENTE: Twenty-five percent! What Shylock, what Arab, what Yankee skinflint is this? (*Aside.*) But what can I do? Since I need the money to print my manifesto, I have to consent to everything. Anything else?

FILERO: (*Pulling out a contract and reading from it.*) "Of the fifteen thousand pesos asked, the lender can only pay out seven thousand, and in place of the remaining eight thousand, the borrower must take furniture, clothing and jewels."

CLEMENTE: What does that mean?

FILERO: Listen. "First: one authentic mariachi costume from the period of Maximillian the First, complete with gold braiding and magnificent sombrero of pure velvet decorated with genuine imitation silver tassels."

CLEMENTE: What does he expect me to do with that—donate it to a museum?

FILERO: Wait. "Second: an authentic hammock from Yucatán woven from the finest henequen fiber used by Mamá Carlota herself during the late Empire Period."

CLEMENTE: Good heavens! What use is that to me?

FILERO: Be patient. "Third: the skin of a burro, now stuffed, used by the late Don Benito Juárez in his escape to the United States of the North during the imperialist siege of Chihuahua."

CLEMENTE: Chihuahua! Where am I going to put that thing?

FILERO: Easy now. "Fourth: a rosary reputed to have been used by Sor Juana Inez de la Cruz, with all its beads, or very nearly all. Fifth: one broken mirror from the Aztec period utilized by Montezuma in divining the arrival of the conquistadores!" And look—"A shard of pottery depicting the cosmic struggle of Huitzilopochtli and his siblings, dating from the time of the Olmecs and unquestionably of great archeological value!"

CLEMENTE: May the revenge of Montezuma fowl his putrid orifices! Have you ever heard of such usury? Isn't he content with the outrageous interest he exacts, without wanting to make me take all the old junk he's collected. I couldn't give it away!

FILERO: He has you by the throat, Señor.

CLEMENTE: ¡Maldita sea mi estampa! This is what young men are reduced to by the cursed avarice of their fathers. And yet people are astonished when sons wish their fathers would die.

FILERO: Why don't you rob him, señor? (*Aside, walking over to another part of the stage.*) Why don't I rob him!

CLEMENTE: (*Reflecting, on his side of the stage.*) I rob him? It would be like robbing myself!

RABIOSO: (*Entering with* DON PROFUNDO, *unaware of* CLEMENTE *or* FILERO.) And so, have you foreclosed on any more widows? Don Quequemáfer?

DON: Oh yes, Don Rabioso, two or three just this morning. And have you quelled any peasant uprisings?

RABIOSO: Oh yes! Every day! (*Laughing and slapping* DON PROFUNDO *on the back.*) And how many young peasant girls have you ravished this month?

DON: Oh, dozens, dozens! And have you executed any political prisoners lately?

RABIOSO: All the time, Don Quequemáfer. (*They laugh and slap each other on the back.*) Seriously though, I'm glad you told me about this meddlesome priest with his sanctimonious preaching. I'll have to keep an eye on him.

DON: Yes, I think you should have him disappeared, and the sooner the better too!

RABIOSO: Now then, about this borrower, he's coming here today.

DON: You invited him to my casa! You know I don't like people coming here tracking up my rugs and breathing my air!

RABIOSO: But this is a gold mine, Don Quequemáfer! The young man is one of those milk-fed puppies who never had to work a day in his life. He's in desperate need of money, and will agree to everything you demand.

DON: But Don Rabioso, are you sure we run no risk? Do you know his name, fortune, family? (FILERO *notices* DON PROFUNDO *and* RABIOSO. *He motions to* CLEMENTE. *They both hide.*)

RABIOSO: No, I haven't met him, although he is highly recommended. His family is very rich, and he will guarantee, if you wish, that his father will die before the year.

DON: And these are the kind of men who will run this country someday? All they do is borrow, borrow, borrow.

RABIOSO: Exactly, you'll have him scraping to pay the interest on the principal in no time! Before you know it, he'll be in debtor's prison! (*They hee-haw and slap each other on the back.*)

FILERO: (*Low. To* CLEMENTE.) Oh no! El Generalísimo is talking to your father!

CLEMENTE: He's always here, working out deals, arrests, foreclosures, evictions ...

FILERO: They're going to send us a la chingada!

RABIOSO: (*Seeing* FILERO.) Aha! There you are!

DON: What's this ...

CLEMENTE: (*To* FILERO.) What's this?

RABIOSO: What's this! Filero, is this the young man who wants to borrow the fifteen thousand pesos? (FILERO *hides.*)

DON: ¡Malcriado! It is you who abandon yourself to such sinful excesses?

CLEMENTE: ¡Vicioso! It is you who deal in such shameful actions?

DON: You want to ruin yourself by such detestable borrowing? Did you not heed the words of Polonius?

CLEMENTE: You seek to enrich yourself by such criminal usury? Have you not learned the lesson of Shylock?

DON: To think you are capable of selling your patrimony!

CLEMENTE: To think you could be one of the moneylenders at the temple!

DON: Get out of my sight, you villain, out of my sight! (*Exit* CLEMENTE.)

RABIOSO: Those young whippersnappers. In my day, men were men, and wheat was wheat. Well then, how goes the business with your daughter? Did you tell her what a hero I am, how I slew hundreds of Frenchmen? How the ladies swoon when I walk by? In short, has she consented to marry me?

DON: She cried tears of joy when I told her.

RABIOSO: Splendid, shall we set a date, for the wedding?

DON: Yes, provided you pay for it.

RABIOSO: Er, I thought it was customary for the father of the bride ...

DON: I also need a new suit of clothes.

RABIOSO: I'll get my, eh, tailor to work right away ...

DON: And the windows need new curtains.

RABIOSO: What! I'm supposed to pay for the blasted curtains as well!

DON: (*Looking out the window.*) My dear loyal servants have been complaining about their dilapidated living quarters ... don't you think those huts need remodeling?

RABIOSO: Surely, you're not suggesting that I ...

DON: And those fields laying fallow? I'm going to need money to plant my orchards. I know you'll want to assist your future father-in-law with a generous loan ... at no interest ... payable in fifty years ... (RABIOSO *coughs, sputters, chokes. Turns red.*) There, there, Don Rabioso, don't fret. After all, you're marrying Elisa and some day this will be all yours.

RABIOSO: But you're burdening me with debt! I'll die before my time! (*They exit arguing.*)

FILERO: (*Popping up from his hiding place.*) Whew, that was a close call. (*Enter FANNY.*)

FANNY: Is the master of the house in?

FILERO: Fanny! What are you doing here?

FANNY: I have a little business with him regarding my niece, for which I hope to be well compensated.

FILERO: Ah! You'll be very lucky if you get anything from Quequemáfer.

FANNY: I thought his name was "Cacamáfer."

FILERO: Oh, don't call him that! That's what they say behind his back. His name is "Quequemáfer," as in "keke."

FANNY: Ah, like a "cake."

FILERO: That's what I said, "keke."

FANNY: What a strange name. It's sounds so foreign.

FILERO: Don Profundo is from Monterrey—where people have a reputation for being stingy.

FANNY: Profundo ...

FILERO: Yes, his dear wife, God rest her soul, used to call him "Profundito." (*They laugh.*) His father had three sons who told them, "when I die, I want each of you to put fifty gold pesos in my coffin." They promised, and each went their separate ways. When the old man died, the son who had gone to South America dutifully deposited fifty gold pesos in the casket. The one who had gone to North America did the same. Cacamáfer, who had stayed in Monterrey, wrote a promissory note for 150 gold pesos and kept the change!

FANNY: But I have a secret for finding men's soft spots.

FILERO: But, Fanny, he can out codo the codoest codo in all Cododom. Ay, here he comes! I can hear the pennies jingling in his pocket. ¡Adiós! (*Exit* FILERO.)

DON: (*Enter* DON PROFUNDO.) Señora Fanny—thank you so much for coming.

FANNY: Don Cacamáfer, how well you look! You are the very picture of health!

DON: Who? I?

FANNY: I've never seen such a fresh and sparkling complexion.

DON: Really?

FANNY: I know men of thirty who look older than you.

DON: I'm over sixty.

FANNY: What is sixty? A mere trifle! You're like the maguey plant who must be allowed to grow and attain full size before its sweet nectar is removed.

DON: Oh, well!

FANNY: Just look at you. You're the type that will live to be one hundred.

DON: Do you really think so?

FANNY: Let me see your hand. My goodness! Don Cacamáfer!

DON: It's Que-que-má-fer.

FANNY: What a life line! Look how far it goes!

DON: What does that mean?

FANNY: I said a hundred, but you'll survive to one hundred and twenty!

DON: Is it possible?

FANNY: They'll have to club you to death. You'll bury your children and your children's children.

DON: So much the better! Now then, have you persuaded your niece to marry me?

FANNY: Oh yes! She received the proposition with pleasure and promised to come and sign the marriage contract this very night.

DON: Are you sure? Mariana is so young, you know. I'm afraid that a man of my age won't be to her liking.

FANNY: How little you know her! She has a frightful aversion to all young men, and only likes old ones like you, Don Cacamáfer.

DON: The name is Quequemáfer, as in "keke."

FANNY: Quequemáfer, excuse me. She cannot bear the sight of a young man. Nothing delights her more than a handsome old gentleman with a majestic beard. Before she came into your household, she broke off a match when she found out that her lover was only fifty-six and didn't need glasses to sign the marriage contract.

DON: Just because of that?

FANNY: Yes, she likes noses with spectacles on them. And the few pictures she has in her room are not of dashing young men. They are of a stately Columbus, our aging reformer Benito Juárez, a graying Presidente Porfirio Díaz.

DON: If I had been a woman, I wouldn't have liked young men either.

FANNY: Who does? They're just show-offs who make you envy their complexions.

DON: Yes, with their falsettoes and their little puffs of beard like chick feathers.

FANNY: They are nothing compared to you, Cacamáfer!

DON: Queque ...

FANNY: (*To the audience.*) Now, here is a man!

DON: You find me attractive?

FANNY: Stunning! Whenever I see your portrait I get weak in the knees. Let me see you walk. (*To the audience as he walks.*) Here is a figure as graceful and strong as a jaguar, with the noble bearing of an eagle.

DON: There's nothing the matter with me except for an occasional catarro. (*He coughs.*)

FANNY: Your catarro is not unbecoming, since you cough with such grace.

DON: Fanny, I'm giving a small dinner for El Generalísimo this evening and I want to invite you and Mariana. (*Beat.*) Feel free to eat before you come.

FANNY: (*Aside.*) Of course, we wouldn't want to starve to death once we're here. (*To* DON.) Don Cacamáfer, some bandidos came down from the mountains and robbed all of the stock from my store last week.

DON: Oh, what a pity! Have you reported it to El Generalísimo?

FANNY: Yes, but all I need is a little loan to start up again. (DON *frowns.*) You would not believe how pleased she will be to see you. (DON *smiles.*) How admirable an effect on her your old-fashioned collar will have. But above all, she will be charmed by your quaint pantalones.

DON: I am delighted.

FANNY: Cacamáfer, I'll be ruined and forced to live on charity! (DON *frowns.*) I wish you could see her eyes light up when I talk to her of you. (DON *smiles.*) Her face beams with joy at the future that awaits her.

DON: I must leave now, a most urgent business.

FANNY: (*Falling dramatically on the floor.*) I'll die like a dog in the streets! (DON *Frowns.*)

DON: ¡Adiós!

FANNY: The bandidos ... !

DON: There! Someone is calling me! (DON *Exits.*)

FANNY: (*Getting up and brushing herself off. This was obviously an act.*) The devil take you, rat face! Oh, I'll get even with him, you'll see! (*Exit* FANNY.)

CLEMENTE: (*Entering with* VALENTÍN *in a heated discussion. He holds the manifesto in his hand.*) I agree with you in principle, but can't concur with your methods.

VALENTÍN: So what do you suggest we do—wait for life in the hereafter?

CLEMENTE: One of our Mexican philosophers, Vasconcelos, wants to mount a literacy campaign. Authors like Homer, Plato, Aristotle will be disseminated among the people.

VALENTÍN: But I already told you—they don't know how to read! The government hasn't built any schools in years. The poor children have to work in order to eat.

CLEMENTE: Exactly, without a literate society, there can be no real Revolution. We need to convene a congress to elect our own leaders.

VALENTÍN: A congress! El Generalísimo would have us all arrested!

CLEMENTE: And at some point you have to hold general elections.

VALENTÍN: General elections! Who would dare to run against your father and his ruling clique ...

CLEMENTE: Why, someone like ...

VALENTÍN: They would have us all shot!

CLEMENTE: Valentín, what if ... I ran against them!

VALENTÍN: What? You!

CLEMENTE: Yes, me! Why not? They wouldn't have me shot!

VALENTÍN: I wouldn't be too sure of that. They'll never give in to the power of the ballot. (*Pulling out a revolver.*) This is the only thing they understand!

CLEMENTE: Valentín, put that away! They have bigger and more powerful weapons, and a vast army to do their bidding.

VALENTÍN: We too are building a vast army, Clemente.

CLEMENTE: No, Valentín, the pen is mightier than the sword. I'll prove it to you! Look, here is the manifesto!

VALENTÍN: (*Grabbing it.*) That was fast! What does it say?

CLEMENTE: A call for reform! Valentín, we could run together on the same ticket. The people will vote for us.

VALENTÍN: I don't know ...

CLEMENTE: But we have everything to gain, and a great deal to lose!

VALENTÍN: This will be an exercise in futility.

CLEMENTE: Will you at least try?

VALENTÍN: Very well. But if it fails, we'll do it this way! (*Raising his pistol up in the air.*)

CLEMENTE: Agreed!

VALENTÍN: Agreed! (*They embrace.*) ¡Que viva la Revolución!

CLEMENTE: ¡Hasta la victoria!

VALENTÍN: ¡Venceremos!

CLEMENTE: ¡No pasarán!

VALENTÍN: ¡Patria o muerte! (*They go off together. Curtain.*)

ACT TWO

Enter on stage DON PROFUNDO, VALENTÍN, TAN-TAN, *and* MARUJA.

DON: ¡Bueno, bueno! Come here—here's what I want done for the cena tonight. Maruja, I'll begin with you. (*She approaches, carrying a broom.*) Good, I see you carry your arms with you. You must clean the entire house, but take care not to rub the furniture too hard, or you'll wear it out. In addition, you're assigned to look after the glasses during supper. If they're lost or broken, I shall deduct it from your wages.

MARUJA: (*Aside.*) ¡Viejo tacaño!

DON: Furthermore, I put you in charge of serving the drinks, but only when someone is thirsty. Don't encourage people to drink. Wait until they have asked you at least five times, and always remember to add water to the wine.

MARUJA: (*Aside.*) God forbid anyone should enjoy themselves. (*To* DON.) Shall I serve without my apron, Señor?

DON: Yes, but be careful not to soil your clothes.

MARUJA: Pero, Señor, you know that I have a large hole in the back of my vestido and, when I bend over, people can see my calzones. (*Bending over to show the holes in her underwear.*)

DON: Ahhmmm, keep that side discreetly to the wall and show them only your, eh, best side. (DON *shows her how to walk with her back to the wall.*) Tan-Tan, you're next.

TAN-TAN: Oiga, Señor, do you wish to speak to your coachman or your cook, for I am both?

DON: To both of you.

TAN-TAN: Which one first?

DON: The cook.

TAN-TAN: Un momento, por favor. (*Puts on his cook's cap.*) ¡Para servirle!

DON: I am to give a cena tonight.

TAN-TAN: (*Aside.*) ¡Qué milagro!

DON: Can you serve us something good?

TAN-TAN: Sí, señor. With pleasure.

DON: Tell me, what do we need?

TAN-TAN: (*Aside.*) Mucho dinero.
DON: There will be ten people, but provide only for six. When there's enough for six, there's plenty for ten.
TAN-TAN: Yes, of course. Hmmmm. Well, we'll need at least two good soups, and five main dishes ...
DON: Hold on!
TAN-TAN: Then salads ... deserts ...
DON: That's enough to feed an entire army!
TAN-TAN: ... five fine wines ...
VALENTÍN: (*To* DON PROFUNDO.) Excuse me, Señor. (*To* TAN-TAN.) What kind of service is this? It's easy to provide a feast with lots of money, but a clever cook can arrange good fare with just a little cash.
TAN-TAN: Bueno, señor mayordomo. Since you are so smart, why don't you take my place and create a miracle like Christ when he multiplied the fish?
DON: Quiet! Like Valentín said, how can we serve plenty for nothing?
TAN-TAN: First, a good mole poblano ...
DON: (*Putting his hand over* TAN-TAN'*s mouth.*) You're eating up all my money!
TAN-TAN: Cabrito al pastor ...
DON: (*Both hands on* TAN-TAN'*s mouth.*) That's enough!
TAN-TAN: (*As he struggles with* DON.) Chiles rellenos ...
VALENTÍN: Do you want to kill everyone of consumption? Has Don Profundo invited people here to have them suffer a stroke? Do you know what a big problem obesity is?
TAN-TAN: Then, why is everyone dying of hunger around here?
VALENTÍN: Moderation is the word. Remember, "One should eat to live and not live to eat."
DON: Well said! I'm going to have that sentence engraved in gold letters above the mantelpiece of my dining room. "One should not eat to death when one could die of living."
VALENTÍN: Don't worry about the cena, señor, leave everything to me.
TAN-TAN: Less trouble for me!
DON: We should have things people don't eat much of, and which will fill them up quickly. A rather fatty pot of frijoles, and plenty of tamales stuffed with masa. Get those old tortillas and make some chilaquiles out of them.
VALENTÍN: Leave everything to me.
DON: Perhaps a nice bean dredge soup. And now, Tan-Tan, we must ready the horse and carriage.

TAN-TAN: Un minuto. This concerns the coachman. (*Discards cook's hat and don's coachman apparel.*) Now then, you were saying?

DON: We shall drive to the cathedral next Sunday. Therefore, make the coach and horses ready.

TAN-TAN: Your horses, señor? ¡Dios mío! They are not in a fit state to walk, much less drag a carriage. They can't even get up from their straw—they have none! You make them observe such strict fasts, that they are no more than shadows.

DON: What's the matter with them—they never do anything!

TAN-TAN: Because they never do anything is that any reason why they shouldn't eat? It would be far better for them, poor beasts, if they worked hard and were fed accordingly.

VALENTÍN: Tan-Tan is becoming a flojo.

TAN-TAN: Valentín is becoming a metiche.

DON: ¡Ya basta!

TAN-TAN: Señor, I can't stand flatterers. His surveillance over the bread, wine, wood, salt and candles is just so he can butter up to you. It grieves me to hear people talk about you behind your back. For, in spite of myself, I do have a real affection for you and, next to my horses, you are the person I like the most.

DON: Tell me, what do people say behind my back?

TAN-TAN: Oh, señor, it would make you very angry.

DON: No it wouldn't, go ahead, tell me.

TAN-TAN: You'll be angry at the bearer of the message.

DON: No, no. I really want to know what other people think of me.

TAN-TAN: All right—you asked for it! You are the butt of a thousand jokes, and your stinginess is legend. One person says you wouldn't lend him a light from your candle to light his cigar, because you were afraid it would lose some of its glow. This one tells the story that you once brought a lawsuit against a neighbor's goat for eating your grass. They say your nose is so big because the air is free. They say you save your spittle, so you can drink it later! Shall I go on? You are the laughingstock of the entire world. They never talk about you except by the name of miser, skinflint, cheapskate, codo, tacaño y mezquino!

DON: (*Beating him.*) ¡Idiota! ¡Miserable! ¡Cabrón!

TAN-TAN: Oh, didn't I predict it? I told you it would make you angry.

DON: ¡Hijo de la madre que te parió! (*Exit* DON PROFUNDO.)

TAN-TAN: (*To the audience.*) What are you laughing at? There's nothing funny about a master beating his servant! (*To* VALENTÍN.) No thanks to you, Meester Hotshot!

VALENTÍN: Why are we fighting when we should be working together? After all, we're in the same boat.

TAN-TAN: What do you mean?

VALENTÍN: Quequemáfer makes slaves out of all of us. The only difference between us is that I sleep in the house, while you sleep in the barn. I only flatter him to keep him off guard.

TAN-TAN: (*Aside.*) I knew it! He's one of those insurrectionists! I'll inform on him and get in Don Profundo's good graces again. (*To* VALENTÍN.) You know, you're right. He is a miserable old miser who hoards all his wealth and never gives anything to his servants. What do you propose to do?

VALENTÍN: (*Putting his arm around* TAN-TAN.) Hermano, one day there will be a big rebellion. My brother Pancho will come riding out of the mountains to sweep the exploiters away. Meanwhile, here in the city, we are laying the ground for the coming Revolution. (*Pulling out a little red book.*) See, it's all written here in this book.

TAN-TAN: (*Humoring him.*) You will free all of us miserable peones and hang the rich landlords up by their cojones?

VALENTÍN: ¡Sí, señor! And we'll form cooperatives and work the land together.

TAN-TAN: What! You mean, I can't have my own little ranchito?

VALENTÍN: Well, the idea is to work for the benefit of all, not just a few. (TAN-TAN *makes a face.*) The party, the Revolutionary Party, will be the vanguard for the workers and peasants, and one day we'll institutionalize the Revolution.

TAN-TAN: Institutionalize the Revolution! ¡Ay, caramba!

VALENTÍN: Just think of it, everyone will have the right to vote . . .

TAN-TAN: I know . . . for the Revolutionary Institutionalized Party . . .

VALENTÍN: Well, yes!

TAN-TAN: Wonderful! Splendid! I can't wait for the rosy future you so glowingly describe for us! (*As they exit.*)

MARIANA: (*Entering with* FANNY.) Oh dear, Aunt Fanny, don't make me do this!

FANNY: But Mariana, I'm marrying you off to a wealthy old gentleman who is certain to die any day.

MARIANA: What a horrible thing it is to wish for the death of someone in order to be happy.

FANNY: You should marry him on the condition that he will soon make you a widow. It ought to be one of the articles in the marriage contract. It would be quite rude of him not to die within two months.

MARIANA: No, I can't go through with it, my heart is with someone else.

FANNY: Who, that young someone you told me about? Yes, fair young men bring blush to your cheeks, but holes to your shoes. Dear girl, your mother, God bless her soul, left you in my care and instructed me to see that you were well provided for. What better way to get back at the man who foreclosed on her estate and brought you into his home as a servant?

MARIANA: By marrying him!

FANNY: Yes! Think how you will torture him by spending all his money. Shhhh, here he comes in person. (*Enter* DON PROFUNDO *powdering his face with talcum powder.*)

MARIANA: Fanny, why is he powdering his face?

FANNY: Why do you think? To make himself whiter!

MARIANA: More European! (DON PROFUNDO *notices them and spills the powder all over his coat.*)

FANNY: Why, Don Profundo, I hope we're not interrupting anything!

DON: (*Trying to put the powder away, but only succeeding in spilling more.*) Why no, Fanny, I was, ahmmm, merely freshening up my complexion. The sun does dry it out you know!

FANNY: (*To* MARIANA.) The sun also turns it brown. (*As* DON PROFUNDO *advances towards them.*) I think you missed a spot here on your forehead. It's what we Mexicans call "having a nopal on your forehead."

DON: A cactus on the forehead?

FANNY: Yes, we say that one looks so Mexican he has a cactus stamped on the forehead.

DON: Oh! How interesting! (*Putting on his glasses and studying* MARIANA.) Well, Mariana, you may be Mexican, but you don't really look Mexican.

MARIANA: (*Aside.*) What a beast!

DON: Don't be offended if I come to you wearing spectacles. It's just that I've never seen you up so close. You're always working upstairs and I've never really had a chance to inspect you.

MARIANA: (*To* FANNY.) He acts as if he were buying a horse!

DON: (*To* FANNY.) Fanny, your niece displays, I think, no joy in seeing me.

FANNY: It's just that she's overcome by your noble visage. Besides, good girls aren't supposed to display what their hearts feel.

DON: You're right. (*To* MARIANA.) Here, my little enchilada, is Elisa, who greets you as my wife to be.

ELISA: (*Entering.*) Doña Mariana. I am glad you will be taking your rightful place in our home.

MARIANA: Thank you, Elisa, you are so kind.

DON: My, Elisa. you're getting tall. But then, weeds do flourish.

MARIANA: (*To* FANNY.) What a repulsive man!

DON: What is my beautiful quesadilla saying?

FANNY: That she finds you charming.

DON: Why, thank you, adorable chile pepper!

MARIANA: (*To* FANNY.) What a monster!

FANNY: She says you cut quite a handsome figure.

DON: My tasty taco, I am so flattered.

MARIANA: (*Aside.*) I can't go through with this!

FANNY: She swoons at the sight of you.

DON: Oh, enough! And now, here comes Clemente to greet you!

MARIANA: Oh, Clemente!

FANNY: (*Aside.*) So this is the young man she fell in love with!

CLEMENTE: Doña Mariana, although my father could not have made a better choice, I cannot rejoice in the plan to make you my stepmother. If I had my way, this marriage would not take place.

DON: What a most impertinent thing to say!

MARIANA: And I must say to you, if you have an aversion to seeing me your stepmother, I feel no less at seeing you my stepson.

DON: There, well said, my precious picadillo. Forgive my son—he is a young fool.

MARIANA: What he has told me is not at all offensive. On the contrary, he pleased me by explaining his real feelings.

CLEMENTE: Mariana, allow me to make amends and tell you that in all of Juárez I have seen no one as charming as you.

DON: That's better.

CLEMENTE: Surely there is no one in all of Mexico who can match your beauty.

DON: Easy now, son.

CLEMENTE: But Father, I am merely complimenting Doña Mariana on your behalf.

DON: Good God, I have a tongue to speak for myself. (*To* MARIANA.) Excuse me, salsa of my existence, for not having offered you some refreshments.

FANNY: (*Aside.*) Perhaps we can turn this new development to our advantage after all.

CLEMENTE: Not to worry, Father. I ordered candy from Celaya, chocolate and a flask of Andalusian wine which I have sent for in your name.

DON: (*Aside.*) He's out of his mind!

CLEMENTE: (*As* DON PROFUNDO *offers his hand to* MARIANA *to get her away from* CLEMENTE.) Doña Mariana, have you ever seen a diamond more sparkling than the one on my father's finger?

MARIANA: It shines brightly, indeed.

CLEMENTE: (*Slipping the ring from his father's finger onto* MARIANA's.) You must see it up close.

MARIANA: It sparkles like the lights of Mexico City.

CLEMENTE: (*As* MARIANA *tries to return the ring.*) Oh no, it is on too beautiful a hand. It is a gift from my father.

DON: ¿Qué?

CLEMENTE: Yes, as in Quequemáfer—the most generous man in all of Mexico. Father, isn't it true that you want Doña Mariana to keep it as a token of your affection?

DON: (*Aside.*) What!

CLEMENTE: There, you see, he indicates to me that you should accept his generosity.

MARIANA: Oh, but I can't ...

CLEMENTE: You must! (*As* DON PROFUNDO *is beside himself.*) He would be insulted if you gave it back.

DON: (*Aside.*) I'll be damned if I don't get it back!

MARIANA: This is too ...

CLEMENTE: He has dozens of rings.

DON: (*Aside.*) Cursed scoundrel!

CLEMENTE: See how shocked he is by your refusal?

DON: (*Aside.*) He'll pay for this!

CLEMENTE: Doña Mariana, you are making my father angry with me.

DON: ¡Malcriado!

CLEMENTE: Please, take it, he begs you!

FANNY: My Lord, what a fuss! Keep the ring since Don Cacamáfer is so set on your having it.

MARIANA: Thank you very much, Don Cacamáfer, your generosity knows no bounds.

DON: The name is Quequemáfer, as in "keke."

MARUJA: (*Entering.*) Señor, there is un hombre here who wishes
to speak to you.

DON: Tell him to go away, can't you see I'm busy?

MARUJA: He says he has some contracts for you to sign ...

DON: Later.

MARUJA: ... and a list of new revenues to discuss.

DON: (*To* MARIANA.) I shall return in the blink of an eye. My
little "frijole."

CLEMENTE: While we're waiting, father, I'll be here entertaining
Doña Mariana.

DON: (*Aside.*) Impertinent son! Has he set out to ruin me! (*Exit*
DON PROFUNDO *and* MARUJA. *Enter* ELISA.)

CLEMENTE: At last—we are alone!

ELISA: Mariana, my brother has confided to me the love he feels
for you and I am deeply sympathetic.

MARIANA: And I have just been told of the deep love you feel
for Valentín.

FANNY: What a fine kettle of fish!

CLEMENTE: (*Getting on his knees.*) Dearest Mariana, if you think
me worthy of you, then I propose marriage in front of
these witnesses. I have no money, as you can see by the
actions of my skinflint father. But I promise you a new
life after the Revolution!

FANNY: What Revolution?

CLEMENTE: The Mexican Revolution! There's no stopping it,
Fanny. We're already organizing the people.

FANNY: You, a Cacamáfer ...

CLEMENTE: The name is Quequemáfer.

FANNY: Excuse me, a Quequemáfer, organizing for the Revolution!

CLEMENTE: Yes, it encompasses all social classes. I only hope
we can effect a peaceful change.

FANNY: I don't believe what I'm hearing!

MARIANA: Dearest Clemente, I accept your offer and willingly
join in helping you to reconstruct a new society. (*They
embrace.*)

FANNY: Oh, you're both mad. Deep sighs and revolutionary zeal
don't pay the bills.

ELISA: (*As* VALENTÍN *enters.*) And Valentín and I are also planning to get married!

FANNY: Double folly!

VALENTÍN: No, a double wedding!

MARIANA: Aunt Fanny, you'll help us, won't you?

ELISA: You won't tell our father, will you?

FANNY: My heart goes out to you children, although I wish I
could say the same for my pocketbook. But we have to
undo what we have done. Elisa, what about the claim
Resbaloso has on you?

ELISA: He means absolutely nothing to me!

VALENTÍN: And I will fight for her honor!

FANNY: Very well, I'll help you! (*They gather around and thank
her.*) Now, about this Revolution, Clemente, what's going
to happen to us, the small landholders, the independent
shopowners?

CLEMENTE: Your property will be fully respected.

FANNY: But my property was stolen!

VALENTÍN: No, requisitioned. You will be fully reimbursed after
the Revolution.

FANNY: Young man, I want my goods back NOW! (*As* FANNY
silently argues with VALENTÍN.)

CLEMENTE: (*Embracing* MARIANA.) Oh, Mariana, I count the
hours until we can be alone.

DON: (*Entering just as* CLEMENTE *is embracing* MARIANA.)
What! My son embracing his intended stepmother, and
she not objecting! Is there something behind this?

ELISA: Why, here comes Father!

DON: Clemente, I need to speak to you about something.

ELISA: I believe this would be an appropriate time for us ladies
to powder our noses.

DON: By all means, powder, powder. One must keep one's fair
complexion. (*Exit* FANNY, ELISA, MARIANA.) Now
then, Clemente, aside from the idea of her being your
stepmother, what do you think of the lady?

CLEMENTE: What do I think of her?

DON: Yes, of her mind, body, soul.

CLEMENTE: Más o menos.

DON: Be more precise.

CLEMENTE: In all candor, Father, her figure is but average, her
intellect ordinary, and her spirit lacks ardor.

DON: But just now you were lauding her with laurels.

CLEMENTE: Only in your name, to please you.

DON: Then you don't like her?

CLEMENTE: Not at all.

DON: Oh. That's a shame, because I was thinking—my age—her youth. People might look at us askance. I was toying with the idea of giving you Mariana, had you not shown such an aversion to her.

CLEMENTE: To me?

DON: To you.

CLEMENTE: In marriage?

DON: In marriage—with a dowry and all the corresponding accouterments thereof.

CLEMENTE: Listen, it's true that she isn't much to my liking, but to please you, father. I will resign myself to marry her.

DON: What if there was no dowry or accouterments?

CLEMENTE: Still. I would make this extreme sacrifice out of affection for you, Papá.

DON: No, no, a marriage can't be happy if the heart isn't in it.

CLEMENTE: Well, I could work on it.

DON: No, I wouldn't ask that of my own son. Had you a liking for her, I would have had her marry you instead of me. I'll just have to follow my original plan.

CLEMENTE: Look, since things have come to this—I might as well tell you the truth. I have been in love with Mariana since the first day she came into this house. Even now, we were making plans to elope this very ... (*Trying to shut his mouth, wishing he had not said it.*) ... eh, night.

DON: Elope, you say? This very night? Mariana agreed to this?

CLEMENTE: Yes, Father, we love each other dearly.

DON: Well, I'm glad you told me. Now. Do you know what you must do? (*Beat.*) You must cease to pursue the lady I intend for myself!

CLEMENTE: So, this is how you trick me! Very well, since it's come to this, I declare that I will never give up my love for Mariana. Furthermore, we're leaving tonight!

DON: Oh no you're not!

CLEMENTE: Yes, we are. And there's nothing you can do about it.

DON: I'll disown you!

CLEMENTE: Go ahead, you've never given me anything, anyway.

DON: Good, I'll take my money with me to my grave!

CLEMENTE: There won't be anything left for you to take!

DON: Just what do you mean by that!

CLEMENTE: Come the Revolution, you won't have anything left!

TAN-TAN: (*Entering.*) ¡Caballeros, caballeros!

DON: Quick, give me a stick with which to beat this young sapling.

TAN-TAN: What! This to your son? You're not dealing with me, you know.

DON: I never want to see him again!

CLEMENTE: I never want to see him again!

TAN-TAN: What, this to your father?

DON: Tan-Tan, we'll make you a judge in this affair, to prove I'm in the right.

TAN-TAN: Very well.

DON: I have a girl whom I want to marry ... and this pendejo wants her for himself.

TAN-TAN: Oh, that's terrible.

DON: Isn't it wrong for a son to disobey his father in that way?

TAN-TAN: You're right. Let me speak to him. You stay here. (*He goes to* CLEMENTE *on the other side of the stage.*)

CLEMENTE: I love a young lady who returns my affection, and my father comes along and wants to take her away from me.

TAN-TAN: That is clearly wrong.

CLEMENTE: A man of his age—shouldn't he leave marriage to younger people?

TAN-TAN: Absolutely. He must be joking. Let me have a word with him. (*He goes back to* DON PROFUNDO.) Well, your son isn't as difficult as you think. He says he was only momentarily carried away by his burning passions, and that he will submit to your wishes provided that you find him some other beautiful girl to marry.

DON: Ah, in that case, tell him that he can have anyone he wants, except for Mariana.

TAN-TAN: Let me handle it. (*Going to* CLEMENTE.) Well, your father isn't so unreasonable. He is quite willing to let you have the girl provided you apologize and show him the deference a son owes his father.

CLEMENTE: Ah, you may assure him that if he only gives me Mariana, we'll stay here in Juárez and make him a very happy grandfather.

TAN-TAN: (*To* DON PROFUNDO.) He agrees to what you say. He hopes you will have many children with your new bride.

DON: Good. Then, I won't disown him, as long as he obeys me.

TAN-TAN: (*To* CLEMENTE.) Everything's fine. He's going to buy you a big house in the country with lots of servants.

CLEMENTE: I don't care about that. All I want is Mariana.

TAN-TAN: Caballeros, you have only to talk to each other. You were about to bash each other's brains in for want of a little communication.

CLEMENTE: Gracias, Tan-Tan. (*Giving him money.*)

TAN-TAN: A usted, señor.

DON: You have pleased me greatly, Tan-Tan, and that calls for a reward. (DON PROFUNDO *reaches into his pocket as* TAN-TAN *extends his hand, but merely pulls out a handkerchief and blows his nose.*) Vete, vete, you'll be rewarded later.

TAN-TAN: (*Aside.*) In heaven, I suppose. (*He exits.*)

DON: (*Yelling.*) Maruja!

MARUJA: (*Entering.*) ¡Sí, señor!

DON: Maruja, I feel like splurging tonight. I want you to prepare a piñata for the cena.

MARUJA: A piñata, señor? What should I stuff it with—candy or nuts?

DON: Stuff it with old tortilla chips or stale bread. I want the birds to be well fed. Go! (MARUJA *makes a face and exits.*)

CLEMENTE: Perdóname, Papá, for my rude display.

DON: Think nothing of it.

CLEMENTE: It's so good of you to do this.

DON: One must sacrifice for those we love.

CLEMENTE: You're not angry at me?

DON: Not at all, let bygones be bygones.

CLEMENTE: I can't tell you how happy you've made me.

DON: If there's anything in the world you want, just ask.

CLEMENTE: No, you've given me enough in giving me Mariana.

DON: What?

CLEMENTE: I said, Mariana is the best gift you could have given me.

DON: Who gave you Mariana?

CLEMENTE: Why, you did, Father.

DON: Me? I did not. You renounced her.

CLEMENTE: Me? Renounce her?

DON: Yes.

CLEMENTE: Not at all. On the contrary, I hold to her more than ever.

DON: What! You go back on your word!

CLEMENTE: I did no such thing. I would sooner renounce life itself.

DON: Let me at you, wretch! Get out of this house and don't ever return!

CLEMENTE: I've already packed.

DON: I disinherit you!

CLEMENTE: You already did.

DON: I give you my curse.

CLEMENTE: I don't want any of your "gifts!"

DON: The next time I see you you'll be lying in the gutter!

CLEMENTE: The next time I see you you'll be behind bars! (*They exit from opposite directions.*)

RABIOSO: (*Entering behind* ELISA, *who is struggling to get away from him.*) Emmm, Elisa, dearest, a word with you.

ELISA: I have nothing to say to you, Señor Resbaloso.

RABIOSO: But Elisa, mi amor, we are betrothed.

ELISA: I wouldn't marry you if you were the last hombre on earth. (*She turns to leave.*)

RABIOSO: (*Pulling out a golden bracelet.*) A have a little present for you!

ELISA: What's that!

RABIOSO: A golden bracelet.

ELISA: And so?

RABIOSO: It's priceless, like your exquisite wrist, where it belongs! (*Trying to clasp it on.*)

ELISA: You think you can buy me that easily!

RABIOSO: Oh no, it's a gift, from my heart to yours!

ELISA: I don't want anything of yours!

RABIOSO: It's 24 carat gold. Melted down from the treasure of Moctezuma!

ELISA: I couldn't possibly take it!

RABIOSO: (*Clasping it on her wrist.*) Oh, I insist!

ELISA: Very well, but only to prove I am not a mean or vindictive person. I assure you, Señor Resbaloso, this bracelet means nothing. You shall gain no advantage from this!

RABIOSO: Oh, but of course. Wait! There's more! (*Pulling out a string of pearls.*) Look, a necklace of fine pearls from Acapulco!

ELISA: Oh, my goodness, that is impressive!

RABIOSO: Yes, and more so around your adorable little neck! (*Offering it to her.*)

ELISA: You must think I have no shame or pride!

RABIOSO: You'll have this and more, Elisa ... if only ...

ELISA: What?

RABIOSO: You'll be ... (*Clasps the necklace around her neck.*) ... my bride!

ELISA: (*Aside.*) Oh, what am I doing? Selling myself to Resbaloso! Have I betrayed my one true love! (*She takes the pearls and bracelet off, turns as if to give them back, changes her mind, and pockets them.*) I'll think about it. Good-bye! (*She exits, leaving* RESBALOSO *empty-handed. He storms off in a rage.*)

PANCHO: (*Entering with* VALENTÍN.) They arrested the priest and threw him in jail. It's only a matter of time before he starts talking. We have to strike now before it's too late.

VALENTÍN: Whatever you say, my brother.

PANCHO: Forget about this voting and calling congress business. It's too late for that. (*Pulling out the red book.*) Who did you say wrote this little red book?

VALENTÍN: Clemente, the son of Quequemáfer.

PANCHO: The son of Cacamáfer!

VALENTÍN: Yes, he's a brilliant theorist. And he's committed to the ideals of the Revolution.

PANCHO: I can't believe that you allowed yourself to get mixed up with him!

VALENTÍN: He's a good man.

PANCHO: Then why isn't he following orders!

VALENTÍN: He's with us in principal. He only asks, and rightfully so, why so many people must die.

PANCHO: A revolution takes sacrifice! Some of us may have to give up our lives. This is just a game to that pampered rich boy.

VALENTÍN: Pancho, Clemente is a valuable ally who I would rather have as a friend than an enemy. Besides, we have blood ties, I am marrying his sister.

PANCHO: Then talk some sense into him. He must follow orders.

VALENTÍN: Bueno, trust me, I'll handle him.

PANCHO: I warn you, I'll put up with no nonsense from him.

VALENTÍN: I assure you, Clemente is with us 100 percent.

PANCHO: Very well, be ready. Tonight we strike the first blow for liberty.

VALENTÍN: ¡Un abrazo, hermano! (*They embrace and exit.*)

FILERO: (*Entering, hiding something under his zarape.*) ¡Maruja! ¡Maruja! ¡Psssst! ¡Ven acá!

MARUJA: (*Entering, carrying a piñata.*) ¿Qué quieres?

FILERO: ¡Lo hice! I did it!

MARUJA: ¿Que qué?

FILERO: Quequemáfer's money box! I stole it! (*Showing her the money box.*)

MARUJA: Cacamáfer's money box!

FILERO: ¡Mira! (*Showing her the money.*)

MARUJA: Look at all that dinero!

FILERO: Te dije, Maruja, I told you I would cheat, lie, steal, murder for you!

MARUJA: Oh, the master is going to be muy enojado with you.

FILERO: He is no longer our master!

MARUJA: You better put that money back before somebody finds out!

FILERO: Don't you understand, ahora podemos escaparnos from this miserable poverty.

MARUJA: But it's not our dinero.

FILERO: This is money he stole from the pueblo, from the swindles, land deals and high rents he charges.

MARUJA: He's still going to string you up by your cojones.

FILERO: I told you, we'll escape to El Norte, to los Estados Unidos.

MARUJA: ¿Con los gringos? Ay no, I hear they're all Protestants!

FILERO: But don't you realize, this is the answer to all our dreams! Please, come with me!

MARUJA: Bueno pues, I'll go pack.

FILERO: Forget about it, we'll buy everything new! We're leaving right now!

MARUJA: Shhhh, someone's coming!

FILERO: ¡Ay, Dios mío! (*They both run around like chickens with their heads cut off, trying to find a place to stash the money box.*)

MARUJA: Here! No, over there! No! Give it to me! (*Out of desperation, she takes the money box and stuffs it into the piñata.*)

VALENTÍN: (*Entering and taking* FILERO *aside.*) Filero, I'm glad I found you. The uprising is being planned for tonight!

FILERO: Good idea! While Cacamáfer and his cronies are stuffing themselves! Now, if you'll excuse us, we have to ...

VALENTÍN: Listen carefully. You are to ring the church bells at precisely twelve midnight. That will be the signal for the people to take over the hacienda.

FILERO: Wonderful, the exploiters will be passed out drunk. We really have to be ... (*Trying to leave.*)

VALENTÍN: I'm counting no you! Don't fail me. Maruja, give me that piñata so I can string it up.

MARUJA: Pero, I haven't finished stuffing it yet.

VALENTÍN: No matter. (*Taking it away from her.*) Good Lord, what have you got in here—rocks?

MARUJA: But, but, but ...
VALENTÍN: Oh look, here comes Elisa, help her with the suit-
    cases. (*Enter* ELISA *dragging along several large suitcases.*
    FILERO *and* MARUJA *help her bring in several more.*)
ELISA: Valentín, I packed a few things, as you suggested.
VALENTÍN: Good Lord, Elisa, we'll need an entire troop train
    to transport all that baggage. (*To* FILERO.) Go on, take
    them out back.
ELISA: But Valentín, I took only the barest essentials. Oh, before
    I forget, I have something for you! Look! (*Pulling out the
    jewels.*) Jewels for the Revolution!
VALENTÍN: Good God! Where did you get those, Elisa!
ELISA: Let's just say that a little piggly-wiggly gave them to me.
    Use them to buy some cannons or a troop train. Now
    then, are you coming with us?
VALENTÍN: (*Noticing that* FILERO *is also trying to take the pi-
    ñata.*) No, Elisa. I must stay and fight. (*Snatching the
    piñata away from* FILERO.) Go on, I'll take that. (*To*
    FILERO.) Hurry, the guests are arriving! (*Exit* FILERO
    and MARUJA.)
ELISA: But, Valentín, you're not a fighter, you're a lover.
VALENTÍN: But my duty is to my country.
ELISA: (*Embracing him.*) No, your duty is to me!
VALENTÍN: You're tempting me.
ELISA: (*Kissing him.*) Nothing must ever keep us apart.
VALENTÍN: I am weakening. (*Kiss.*) My revolutionary principles
    are melting. (*Kiss.*)
CLEMENTE: (*Entering.*) Valentín! What's this I hear about an
    uprising!
VALENTÍN: They arrested the priest. El Generalísimo is torturing
    him in the presidio!
CLEMENTE: I fear the worst!
VALENTÍN: If we don't strike now, we may never again have the
    element of surprise again.
CLEMENTE: But you gave me your word!
VALENTÍN: I'm sorry, but orders are orders.
CLEMENTE: But don't you see how this reckless conduct will
    cause many men to lose their lives!
VALENTÍN: It's too late, Clemente. The die is cast. Now, are you
    with us or against us?
CLEMENTE: (*Reluctantly.*) You know I'm with you.
VALENTÍN: I knew I could count on you! (*They embrace.*)
ELISA: Shhh, let's leave! I hear my father coming! (*They exit.*)

DON: (*Entering from the garden.*) Thieves! Insurrectionists! Communists! I am lost! They've cut my throat, boiled me in oil, drawn and quartered me—stolen my banknotes!!! Where is he? Where could he be? Where did he go? There. Here. Everywhere. Nowhere. (*Noticing his shadow on the wall.*) Ah, what's that! Stop! (*Seizing his own arm.*) Give me back my money! Oh! It's me! Oh, I've stolen my own money. Eh, gads, I'm going insane, crazed, loco. My mind is in a turmoil. I don't know who I am! My poor money. Old friend. Lover! I am lost without you! They have deprived me of my only joy in life. Without you I am dead! Life is impossible. They might as well dig a hole and bury me right here in the ground. Can no one bring me back to life by telling me who took my money? Eh? What's that? (*To the audience.*) What are you saying? What are you looking at? Are you laughing at me? Did one of you take my money? You all look suspicious to me! Officers! Policemen! ¡Guardias! ¡Señor Presidente! Lock these people up! Detain them! They've stolen my money! I'll have everybody shot—and if I don't get my money back, I'll shoot myself! (*Exit* DON PROFUNDO.)

TAN-TAN: (*Entering with the piñata under his arm.*) Right this way. Generalísimo, right this way.

RABIOSO: (*Entering, with a pistol in his hand.*) Make way. The forces of public order have arrived. (*To the audience.*) If there are any thieves out there, they might as well give up now. I have ways of making you talk. (*To* TAN-TAN.) How much money was lost?

TAN-TAN: I heard my master say ten thousand in cash.

RABIOSO: Such a large sum to have in the house.

DON: (*Entering.*) Ah, there you are!

RABIOSO: Don Profundo, why did you hide the money here in the house? You could have kept it in the bank and earned five percent interest.

DON: I don't trust banks.

RABIOSO: But you own a bank.

DON: There are rats in the vaults and they gnaw away at my precious banknotes.

RABIOSO: Well, no matter. My policía always get their man. By the way, I had that meddlesome priest arrested today. I suspect that he is in league with the insurrectionists and it is only a matter of time before he "confesses." (*Laughs at his joke.*) Get it?

DON: Yes, yes, but first let's find my money box!

RABIOSO: Tell me, whom do you suspect?

DON: Everyone. I want you to arrest the entire city and the suburbs.

RABIOSO: Don't worry, they won't escape. I have men posted at all the gates and bridges. Who shall we start with first?

DON: (*Pointing to* TAN-TAN.) This one! Now, give me back my money or I'll have you hanged!

RABIOSO: Don't abuse him. He's the one who informed me of the theft.

DON: There, that proves he's guilty.

TAN-TAN: If I was guilty, don't you think I would be in hiding?

DON: A clever ploy. Now, out with it, or I'll have you boiled in oil.

TAN-TAN: I do know one thing.

DON: What?

TAN-TAN: Valentín is an insurrectionist.

DON: Valentín!

RABIOSO: An insurrectionist?

DON: You're sure?

TAN-TAN: I'm sure.

RABIOSO: He's sure.

DON: Valentín, who seemed so faithful?

TAN-TAN: His brother is Pancho Pérez.

RABIOSO: The notorious bandido!

TAN-TAN: Yes, the notorious revolucionario who steals from the rich and gives to the poor.

DON: (*To* TAN-TAN.) How do you know that?

TAN-TAN: Valentín tried to get me to join the Revolution. But since I am so loyal to my master, I just went along to learn of his plans so I could come back and tell you.

DON: What proof do you have that he took my strong box?

TAN-TAN: I saw him with the strong box!

RABIOSO: Describe it.

TAN-TAN: Well, it was a very strong box. It was very large.

DON: The one they stole from me was small.

TAN-TAN: Yes, yes, that's what I meant. A small box considering the large amount of money that was in it.

RABIOSO: What color was it?

TAN-TAN: What color. The color is ... a certain color. I can't express it. Wouldn't you say it's blue?

DON: No, red.

TAN-TAN: That's it, a reddish blue!

DON: There's no doubt about it. It fits the description perfectly. Good Lord, you can't trust any of the hired help these days. I demand his immediate arrest, torture and execution.

RABIOSO: Where is this Valentín?

TAN-TAN: I last saw him with Señorita Elisa in the dining room.

RABIOSO: I will go detain him forthwith and commence to apply fully the rigors of the law. (*Exit* RABIOSO.)

DON: Tan-Tan, my faithful servant. Once again you have done me a great service. Here is your reward! (*Reaching into his coat pocket,* DON PROFUNDO *pulls out a lock of hair and hands it to* TAN-TAN.)

TAN-TAN: What's this?

DON: I know how much you like me, so here is a lock of my very own hair.

TAN-TAN: Señor, I don't know what to say.

DON: My hair is rapidly being lost to the years.

TAN-TAN: I am most profoundly moved. (*Beat.*) If you'll excuse me, señor, I have to put up this piñata.

DON: Ah, here comes that despicable poltroon!

RABIOSO: (*Dragging in* VALENTÍN.) He tried to vamoose, but the long arm of the law collared him.

DON: Blackguard! I know everything! You had better come clean.

RABIOSO: Yes, and save me the trouble of extracting a confession by force.

VALENTÍN: What am I accused of?

DON: Of taking what is rightfully mine!

VALENTÍN: (*Aside.*) Surely they're not talking about the rebellion! (*To* DON.) Oh, that! Well, I certainly can't deny that!

TAN-TAN: (*Aside.*) Could I have guessed right?

VALENTÍN: Don Profundo, I implore you not to be angry and to listen to my motives. After all, the offense is pardonable.

TAN-TAN: (*Aside.*) They'll hang him up like this piñata! (*Stringing up the piñata.*)

DON: Pardonable! You thief! A desecration like that, a horrible abomination!

VALENTÍN: Señor. I do not deserve to be called a thief. You'll see that the harm isn't as great as you make it out to be.

DON: The harm isn't as great as I make it out to be! What! I'm going to have a heart attack! You monster! What drove you to such a vile deed?

VALENTÍN: In brief, one word, love.

DON: (*Aside.*) Love? Love of my pesos!

RABIOSO: Let me put him before the firing squad this instant!

DON: Out with it! Where is my treasure?

VALENTÍN: Why, señor, she is right here in the house.

DON: My treasure still here? You have not tampered with it?

VALENTIN: No, señor, I have too much respect for her. You wrong us. I burn with a pure and holy ardor.

DON: (*Aside.*) He burns for my strong box?

VALENTÍN: I could never think of profaning her. I respect her as I would the Virgin of Guadalupe!

DON: (*Aside.*) My money box like the Virgin of Guadalupe?

VALENTÍN: No foul thoughts have profaned the light those beautiful eyes have inspired in me.

DON: (*Aside.*) My money box's beautiful eyes? He talks like a lover about his mistress. What in the devil are you talking about?

VALENTÍN: Why, your daughter, of course! We are to be married.

DON: My daughter getting married to you!

RABIOSO: My bride getting married to you!

DON: Another disgrace. You are a seducer, as well as a thief!

RABIOSO: What an insult—this calls for a duel! (*Taking off his gloves and slapping* VALENTÍN *across the face.*)

VALENTÍN: Señor, I warn you! You are making me angry! (RABIOSO *slaps him again.*) I am getting angrier! (DON PROFUNDO *joins in the slapping.*) I am furious! Enraged!

ELISA: (*Entering with* MARIANA *and* FANNY.) Father, please, Valentín saved me from the burning deserts of Chihuahua. I owe him my life ...

DON: Shameless hussy! It would have been better for me had he let you perish in the sand dunes. (*Slapping* VALENTÍN *again.*)

RABIOSO: Elisa! I, the bravest man in all of Mexico, intend to do battle for your hand!

ELISA: Father, please!

DON: To think that you let yourself fall in love with this thief, this indio patas rajadas!

VALENTÍN: Señor, you insult me. I am not a thief. I have Indian blood in my veins, yes, like you and him (*Pointing to* RESBALOSO.) and all us Mexicanos!

DON: How dare you ...

RABIOSO: I shall return ...

DON: Can't you tell I am of pure Castillian stock?

RESBALOSO: I just happen to have a pair of dueling pistols in my carriage. (*Aside.*) Little does he know I am the best marksman in all of North America! (*He exits.*)

DON: (*Shots are heard off stage.*) What's that! Tan-Tan, go see who's making that racket. (*Exit* TAN-TAN.) Now then, are you going to tell me what you did with my money?

VALENTÍN: Señor, I do not know what you are talking about!

ELISA: Papá, I beg of you!

DON: No, he shall pay for this—with his life! (*Choking* VALENTIN, *a furious fight ensues, enter* TAN-TAN, MARUJA, *etc.*)

FANNY: (*Trying to restrain him.*) Don Cacamáfer, please!

MARIANA: Yes, for the love you claim to hold for me, have mercy!

RABIOSO: (*Entering.*) Don Profundo, let go! I have the right to kill him first!

DON: No! He stole my money! (*Grappling with* RABIOSO.)

RABIOSO: He stole my bride!

FANNY: (*Pulling them apart.*) Stop it, both of you!

RABIOSO: (*Extracting dueling pistols.*) Choose your weapon! (*Giving* VALENTÍN *a pistol.*) Aha! (*Aside to* DON PROFUNDO.) I gave him the one loaded with blanks.

DON: (*Aside.*) Excellent. Let the duel commence. I shall be your second.

PANCHO: (*Entering.*) And Valentín shall be my second.

DON: Fine! (*Beat.*) Who are you?

PANCHO: Pancho Pérez.

VALENTÍN: Elisa, this is my brother! Pancho, this is my bride to be!

PANCHO: (*Bowing deeply.*) Un placer, señorita ... (*Kissing her hand.*)

RESBALOSO: (*Shaking in his boots.*) Pancho Pérez! The infamous ...

DON: (*His voice wavering.*) ¡Bandido!

VALENTÍN: ¡Revolucionario!

PANCHO: (*Pulling out two pistols.*) Shall we start the duel?

VALENTÍN: By all means.

PANCHO: Here, little brother, why don't I take your place?

VALENTÍN: Gracias, hermano.

DON: Well, good luck with your duel, Rabioso. (*Starting to exit.*) I just remembered I have to go over some very pressing accounts.

RABIOSO: (*Holding him back.*) Oh no you don't, you got me into this.

DON: (*Trying to break free.*) But I abhor violence. I'm a pacifist!

RABIOSO: You fight him! (*Stage business with each of them trying to get the other to face* PANCHO.)

DON: After you!

RABIOSO: No, you may do the honors.

PANCHO: (*Back to back with* RABIOSO.) Are you ready? Twenty paces, agreed? Uno, dos, tres ...

RABIOSO: (*Dropping the pistol.*) Oh, please, señor, I suddenly feel very faint.

PANCHO: I'll wager you'll need a physician before long. (*Continuing to pace.*) Siete, ocho, nueve ...

RABIOSO: I pray you, sir!

PANCHO: May you have a long life in the hereafter.

RABIOSO: I—I renounce all my claims to Elisa!

PANCHO: Good. (*Still pacing.*) Trece, catorce, quince ...

RABIOSO: I renounce all claims to being the greatest Generalísimo alive!

PANCHO: Then, you obviously have no use for those ridiculous trappings. (*Motioning that he should take off his uniform.*)

RABIOSO: My uniform? You want me to expose myself!

PANCHO: (*Shooting his pistol into the air.*) Off with it! (*El Generalísimo rips off his jacket, revealing a bra underneath.*)

RABIOSO: (*Down on his knees.*) Have mercy! I surrender!

PANCHO: Now, for the next opponent! (*Stepping back to back with* DON PROFUNDO.)

DON: (*As* CLEMENTE *enters.*) I renounce all my claims to Mariana!

CLEMENTE: I heard that!

PANCHO: (*Starting to count off the paces.*) Uno, dos, tres ...

DON: And I give her as a bride to my son Clemente.

PANCHO: (*Still pacing.*) Yes, what else ...

DON: They shall be married this very night!

PANCHO: (*Pacing.*) Good, keep going ...

DON: And I shall pay for the wedding!

PANCHO: Nothing more? (*He stops, whirls around.*)

DON: I shall also pay for the wedding of my daughter and Valentín! (PANCHO *points his gun at* DON PROFUNDO.) And provide for a sumptuous feast! For all the guests—and servants!

PANCHO: (*Placing the gun directly at* DON PROFUNDO's *head.*) What do you say to giving up all your money for the good of the Revolution! (*Cocking the trigger.*)

DON: What! My money for my life!

ELISA: Give it up, Papá, give it up! (*Pointing the gun away from her father's head.*)

DON: (*Pointing the gun back at his head.*) No, no, shoot me, shoot me! I can't live without it!

PANCHO: Blast you, old devil! (*Beat.*) We'll spare your life, but take your money! (PANCHO *shoots his guns several times into the air, striking the piñata. Bills flutter to the ground.*)

TAN-TAN: ¡Ajúa! It's raining pesos!

FANNY: ¡Qué lindo, una fiesta!

PANCHO: Yes, a fiesta of bullets! A fiesta of bullets! (PANCHO *shoots his gun off again. More bills flutter down, creating pandemonium. QUEQUEMÁFER runs around trying to catch the bills, but everyone beats him to it. Mariachi music is heard. As the lights dim, the festive air turns cold. PANCHO takes CLEMENTE aside.*) Now then, a few words with you, Clemente. How do you feel about everyone sharing your father's money?

CLEMENTE: He had so much of it. Besides, most of it belonged to the pueblo.

PANCHO: How about you? Don't you want any of the money?

CLEMENTE: Money doesn't interest me.

PANCHO: You don't have any money hidden away?

VALENTÍN: (*Overhearing what his brother is saying.*) His father left him with nothing.

CLEMENTE: That's right, I'm as poor as the next man.

PANCHO: What are you going to do now?

CLEMENTE: Organize a constitutional convention. Mexico deserves to have the first truly free elections in it's history. The people have the right to choose their own governors.

VALENTÍN: He's right, Pancho. This is the twentieth century. We have to start talking and stop shooting.

PANCHO: And you're going to go along with him, little brother?

VALENTÍN: Yes, we're going to build the new Mexico!

PANCHO: Oh no you're not! (PANCHO *Pulls out his pistol and arrests CLEMENTE. The music stops playing. Silence.*)

VALENTÍN: What are you doing!

PANCHO: Arresting him for counter-revolutionary activity!

CLEMENTE: By who's authority!

PANCHO: One more word from you and I'll have you shot!

VALENTÍN: Why don't you arrest his father instead?

PANCHO: (*Pointing to CLEMENTE.*) Because he's the one with the dangerous ideas!

FANNY: You bully! You're no different from Resbaloso!

MARIANA: (*Trying to stop* PANCHO.) You let him go!

VALENTÍN: You're out of your mind!

PANCHO: (*To* VALENTÍN.) You're being very naive, little brother! Don't you see, he's a Quequemáfer!

VALENTÍN: You might as well arrest me too!

PANCHO: (*Threatening* VALENTÍN *with his pistol.*) If you betray us, I will! (PANCHO *pushes* VALENTÍN *and starts leading* CLEMENTE *away.*)

VALENTÍN: If this is the Revolution, I don't want any part of it! (PANCHO *and* CLEMENTE *exit.*) Do you hear me!

MARIANA: Valentín, please stop him, do something!

VALENTÍN: (*In despair.*) I can't! I can't! (*A shot rings out off stage. Everyone looks at each other in shock.* MARIANA, FANNY *and* ELISA *race off stage. The servants gather in a cluster commenting, as always, on the action. Rigor mortis has set in on El Generalísimo.*)

ELISA: He's dead! Clemente is dead!

VALENTÍN: (*Pulling out his pistol and racing off stage followed by* ELISA.) ¡Demonio! ¡Bestia! (*More shots are heard. The servants scatter.*)

DON: Oh no, my son! My country! My life! (DON *starts to wander off in the direction of the shooting. A stray banknote catches his eye. He stops, kneels, picks it up and holds it high. A cry, something between laughter and sorrow, escapes his throat. Slow fade.*)

THE END

Pancho Diablo

CHARACTERS*

MARIACHI
CHISMOSA
VÍBORA
MACHO
BRUJA
COYOTE
NOCHE BUENA
PANCHO DIABLO
SAN PEDRO
HOMBRE
MUJER
BORDER PATROL
VOICE
DIOS (THE FATHER)
CHUY (THE SON)
POPE PAPA
OPERATOR
DIABLO PUPPET

SCENES

EL INFIERNO
LA TIERRA
EL CIELITO LINDO

*Certain parts may be double cast

.... PROLOGUE ....

Enter MARIACHI *to sing.*

Corrido

Este es el corrido del gran Pancho Diablo
señor que era dueño de una gran cantina
donde iban los machos a tomar tequila
a vender mujeres y a oler cocaína.

Ahí están las chulas retecoquetonas
y las abuelitas pidiendo limosnas
cinco policías buscando mordidas
sacándole el jugo a la mala vida.

Bienvenidos todos a esta Gran Cantina
dejen sus pistolas ahí en esa esquina
Señores, digan en cuál vicio
este es el dominio del Señor Dionisio

Welcome to the story of Mr. Pancho Diablo
the founder and owner of La Gran Cantina
where the machos go to drink their tequila
pimp all their women and snort cocaína.

He has every service, he has every vice
He will do his best to keep you satisfied
He has all the ladies, he has all the dice
He will do his best to keep you satisfied

CHORUS:

We'll get you some coca
We'll get you some frías
We have perfumed putas
that work noche y día

Smoke marihuana
shoot some heroína
feel at home amigos
en La Gran Cantina

The curtain rises on the grand spectacle of hell. Smoke and fire. The denizens are preoccupied with their awful passions, general mayhem. BRUJA *and* COYOTE *fight like cats and dogs near the cash register, while* VÍBORA *and* CHISMOSA *casually exchange insults at a table downstage.* MACHO, *meanwhile, sits in a corner stuffing himself with food. A terrible heartrendering shriek is heard from* PANCHO *offstage. Everything stops. Silence. This is followed by screams from* NOCHEBUENA.

CHISMOSA: Uh, uh, Pancho and his girl are at it again. Ain't it terrible?

VÍBORA: You love it, bitch.

CHISMOSA: Fuck-off, asshole!

VÍBORA: (*Bending over.*) Be my guest, wish you could! (VÍBORA *cuts a fart.* CHISMOSA *keels over, playing dead.*)

MACHO: (*Sneaking up behind* BRUJA *and fondling her.*) Hey, Mamasota, get down with your Papasote!

BRUJA: (*Kicking* MACHO *in the groin.*) Bug off, cara de zopilote.

MACHO: (*In great pain.*) That's how I like my viejas ... with ... fire. (*A bag of white powder falls out.*)

BRUJA: (*Giving him another kick.*) I'll chop off your desire!

COYOTE: (*Picking up bag of white powder.*) Hhhmmmmmmmm. I'm going to snort some of this shit and make me "Mister Feel Good."

VÍBORA: Let me see that! (VÍBORA *rips the bag and throws it down on the floor, scattering the powder.*)

COYOTE: ¡Cabrón! What are you doing? That's my breakfast!

MACHO: (*To* VÍBORA.) Why you throw my coke on the floor!

VÍBORA: I just felt like it.

COYOTE: (*Snapping his fingers at* MACHO.) Waste him, pendejo.

MACHO: Muthafucka! Muthafucka! (*Nearly in tears, beating* VÍBORA.)

VÍBORA: ¡Más, más, más! I love it, love it!

CHISMOSA: Cool it, batos, here comes Pancho with his ruca! (*They all move aside as* PANCHO *enters with* NOCHE BUENA. PANCHO *has a tail, horns, hooved feet; fire and smoke comes out of his mouth and ears. In short, he is the very personification of the beast.*)

NOCHE BUENA: What in the hell's gotten into you!

PANCHO: (*To no one in particular.*) You're disgusted!

NOCHE BUENA: Coño, Papi, ¿pero qué te hice you a ti?

PANCHO: You're disgusting. (*To the other* DIABLOS.) You're all disgusting! You make me sick!

NOCHE BUENA: (*To the* DIABLOS.) Pero yo no hice nada, I didn't do nothing.

CHISMOSA: (*To* BRUJA.) I know qué pasó, she gave it away for free!

BRUJA: Why should that bother him? This is La Gran Cantina.

NOCHE BUENA: Liars! ¡Mentirosas! (*To* PANCHO.) Don't believe a word, Papi, you know I love only you.

VÍBORA: (*To* COYOTE.) The problem is she has a heart of gold— just can't say "no."

NOCHE BUENA: (*Starting to cry.*) Sometimes I forget where I am!

COYOTE: Ahhh, you see, that's their fate!

MACHO: He wants a virgen, he gets a whore.

BRUJA: She wants a husband, she gets a pimp.

DIABLOS: (*In chorus.*) Supreme irony!

PANCHO: (*Furiously, fire leaping out of his mouth.*) Which one of you made it with her!

COYOTE: Not me.

BRUJA: Not me.

VÍBORA: I haven't had an erection in years. My fate. (*All eyes focus on* MACHO *whose erection is always "on."*)

MACHO: I couldn't help it, I couldn't help it! She pressed herself upon me! She took advantage of me!

NOCHE BUENA: (*Exiting in tears.*) ¡Ay, mi madre!

PANCHO: (*Pulling out his bull whip.*) ¡Pinches diablos!

COYOTE: (*To* MACHO.) You're going to get it now, pendejo.

VÍBORA: (*Stepping in front of* MACHO.) No, no, he's innocent. I did it, I did it.

PANCHO: Day in, day out. Same old stuff.

COYOTE: Uh, patrón, I just got a brand new shipment of sinners. Will you give the customary welcoming torture?

PANCHO: (*Distracted.*) Chale, Coyote, you go right ahead.

COYOTE: But boss, they're Republicans, Hispanic-American Republicans! (PANCHO *hands* COYOTE *the whip.*) Okay. My pleasure. (*Exits.*)

CHISMOSA: Coño, Papi, you down? Come here, I'll show youse a good time.

PANCHO: What can you show me, Chismosa?

CHISMOSA: Love baby, el amor.

PANCHO: What do you know of love?

CHISMOSA: It's my ... profession.

PANCHO: Obsession ... (*Brushing by her, he turns to the thermometer on the wall.*) Who turned up the thermometer? Six hundred and forty degrees Fahrenheit!

COYOTE: (*Entering with a chain gang of sinners.*) The better to torture the clientele, boss.

PANCHO: I'm burning up in here.

VÍBORA: They buy more beer.

BRUJA: Ay, Pancho, I thought you liked it hot.

PANCHO: I'm sweating like a pig!

COYOTE: Señor, would you like to watch these benditos cristianitos beg for mercy?

PANCHO. I can't take this anymore!

CHISMOSA: What's eating him?

PANCHO: What are you all staring at? Get back to work! (*Flailing them with his whip.*) Go on, get out of here! ¡Cabrones! ¡Hijos de la gran puta! (*They all flee except for* VÍBORA *who is in ecstasy.* PANCHO *has to kick him off. Exit* PANCHO.)

MARIACHI: (*Entering.*) ¡Pues, qué bato! After millenniums of playing the heavy, Pancho was fed up past the point of ya no aguanto. So, he decided to take his complaint directly to the personnel department. (*Exits.*)

PANCHO: (*From a high point on the set, he calls up to* SAN PEDRO.) ¡Oye, San Pedro! Paaaay-drooooo! ¿Estás sordo? Wake up!

SAN PEDRO: (*Entering, rubbing his eyes.*) Now, who the devil could that be?

PANCHO: Soy yo, El Diablo, I want to talk to Dios, it's important.

SAN PEDRO: ¿Que qué? You want to talk to ... Dios! That's impossible! Estás loco. He's very busy. He doesn't want to talk to you. Remember what you did!

PANCHO: That's exactly it. What did I do? I'm the wronged party. Who used me to achieve His goals? Who's the fall guy here? I ought to sue Him!

SAN PEDRO: You're getting out of hand, boy!

PANCHO: ¡Chinga tu madre!

SAN PEDRO: Watcha tu language, ¡hay mujeres presentes! I'm going to send down an archangel to wash your mouth out with soap.

PANCHO: Okay, Peee-drooooo. You listen and you listen good. Tell the Lord I quit!

SAN PEDRO: ¿Que qué? ¿Cómo que vas a quit? You can't quit. It's your destiny.

PANCHO: Tell him to find another chump to take my place.
SAN PEDRO: You're serious, aren't you? Well, I have news for
         you, you're tether doesn't reach very far.
PANCHO: It frayed.
SAN PEDRO: You'll never get past the concertina wire fence.
PANCHO: It has holes in it.
SAN PEDRO: The river!
PANCHO: I've been taking swimming lessons.
SAN PEDRO: You're crazy, this is unheard of. Even if you did
         escape, what would you do, where would you go?
PANCHO: No sé. Maybe I'll join the Hell's Angels. ¿A ti qué te
         importa, anyway?
SAN PEDRO: Listen here, you'll disrupt the whole order of things!
PANCHO: Fine.
SAN PEDRO: The cosmos will collapse!
PANCHO: That's His problem. He made it, let Him fix it.
SAN PEDRO: Wait a minute, Diablo, let's talk things over.

     Ya basta (*Ballad.*)

         PANCHO:

     Ya basta, ya basta, ya basta
     te dije

     My job has not been easy
     boiling in the fires of Hades

     Drinking blood and eating babies
     Every day and every night
     and my diet is a fright
     am I wrong or am I right

     For a million years
     I've been el más chueco
     God has coined me as his opposite
     Like the other side of un espejo

SAN PEDRO:

     That's your job
     that's the reason you were born
     Back to Hell
     Back to Hell where you belong

PANCHO:

I've been his Diablo too long
tell him to shove it
and take these horns!

I no longer have to pay
for the mistake
that I made so long ago
when I rebelled
So I feel the time has come
for me to say
Ya basta, te dije

(PANCHO *unscrews his horns and tail and throws them up to* SAN
PEDRO *who pokes at them with his shoe as though they were dead
rats.*)

SAN PEDRO: Wait a minute! Don't go. Maybe we can work
something out. How about a nice post in Purgatory?
PANCHO: ¡Chale con el Purgatorio!
SAN PEDRO: Well, then, maybe we can open up a branch office
on Pluto! You'll love it there.
PANCHO: Don't insult my intelligence, viejo tapado, agachado,
Tío Taco! (PANCHO *exits.*)
SAN PEDRO: Oh, Christ! This is cataclysmic! I better go tell the
Master right away! (*Exit* SAN PEDRO.)
MARIACHI: (*Entering.*)

Pancho regresó a su Gran Cantina
empezó a empacar su mochila
estaba rodeado por sus sujetos
que esperaban su despedida

MACHO: Oye, boss, ¿a dónde vas?
PANCHO: (*Packing his bags.*) Anywhere, I don't care. I'm taking
the first elevator out of here.
CHISMOSA: Coño, Papi, who's going to add up the bar chips and
collect the money from the tricks at the end of the day?
PANCHO: You are.
BRUJA: Who's going to stoke the furnace to keep things hot?
PANCHO: You can do it.
COYOTE: Wait a minute! Who's going to guide us in the eternal
gang-bang with Dios and his archangels?
PANCHO: I give you full liberty. All of you! Attention! ¡Atención!
(PANCHO *gets up on a table.*) ¡Pintos! ¡Putos! ¡Pen-
dejos! ¡Pelados! ¡Malcriados! ¡Cabrones! ¡Ladrones!

tones! ¡Borrachos! ¡Marijuanos! ¡Banqueros! ¡Sacrista-
nes! ¡Putas! ¡Chismosas! ¡Culeras! ¡Rednecks! ¡E hijos
de la chingada!

¡Adiós Cabrones! (*Huapango.*)

Ya me voy para la tierra
quizás nunca regresaré
voy a vivir una nueva vida
no tan cruel o tan jodida

Este jale fue difícil
necesito vacación
after years of burning souls
I deserve a promoción

Atascados y perdidos
here is the key to hell
to keep you just as miserable
as the very day you fell

Murder, cheat, lie and steal
gástense, no hagan nada
may wrath be your cry
y que se vayan a la chingada

(PANCHO *throws the great key to hell into the crowd, whereupon a tremendous imbroglio ensues.* PANCHO *tries to exit, but
runs into* NOCHE BUENA.)

NOCHE BUENA: Pancho, wait! Take me with you!
PANCHO: I'm sorry, Mami, I've got to do this alone.
NOCHE BUENA: At least tell me where you'll be!
PANCHO: I promise to come back for you! (*He exits.*)
NOCHE BUENA: ¡Cabrón!
MACHO: I get all the beer! And all the drugs! The women are
    mine!
CHISMOSA: No you don't, I don't need a pimp.
VÍBORA: ¡Yo soy el que manda aquí! Look, I have the key! But I
    got the huevos, maricón!
COYOTE: (*Smashing a bottle over* VÍBORA's *head while talking to*
    MACHO.) Shit for brains! You can't fart and chew gum
    at the same time.
BRUJA: (*To* NOCHE BUENA, *as they watch the men fight.*) De-
    cided to return, sugar?

NOCHE BUENA: Once you sign in here, your ass belongs to the house.

BRUJA: Don't you worry, honey. Stick with us, we won't exploit you and use you for your body. (BRUJA *licks* NOCHE BUENA's *ear.*)

CHISMOSA: Coño, hermanas, this place is going to the dogs.

NOCHE BUENA: At least Pancho parcelled out wickedness fairly.

BRUJA: (*Feeling* NOCHE BUENA *up.*) ¡Mujeres! We don't need Pancho or any other macho. Don't you see, we're all victims of machismo.

CHISMOSA: (*Pointing to where the men have just about knocked themselves out.*) Look, the key!

BRUJA: ¡Mujeres! I have a plan that will have those perros eating out of our hand. Sister, go agile like a cat and steal the key. (*Trying to mount* NOCHE BUENA, *as* CHISMOSA *fetches the key. The men are down for the count.*)

CHISMOSA: ¡Aquí está!

BRUJA: At last! The key to the gates of hell!

NOCHE BUENA: Let me touch it ...

BRUJA: (*Holding it higher, out of reach.*) We're going to bring this infierno to a screeching halt.

NOCHE BUENA: Shut down La Gran Cantina?

BRUJA: That's right, S&M torture chamber, furnace, todo!

CHISMOSA: Yeah, let those putos make their own mondongo for breakfast.

NOCHE BUENA: Wait, what about all those lost souls knocking at the front door trying to get in?

BRUJA: Send them back from whence they came.

NOCHE BUENA: ¡Ya veo, una huelga!

CHISMOSA: A strike!

BRUJA: That's right, mujeres! To your brooms! (*The* MUJERES *grab their brooms and encircle the men as they awaken.*)

MACHO: Ay qué cruda, I'll never drink again as long as I live.

COYOTE: ¡Viejas! ¡Pinches viejas! Bring us menudo, mondongo! (*To* VÍBORA.) Ever notice como siempre se te para el bicho en la mañana?

VÍBORA: I wouldn't know.

MACHO: Hmmmmmm, I need a woman. ¡Viejas! I'm hungry!

COYOTE: Hey, where's my key, where's my golden key?

MACHO: My stash man, I can't find my stash. (*Checking the cooler for beer.*) Oh shit, and we're out of beer. Ohhhhhhhhhhh.

BRUJA: (*Holding up the key.*) Looking for this, master?

COYOTE: Pinches viejas, wait until I get my hands on you. Macho, where's your pistola?

NOCHE BUENA: (*Holding up a pistol.*) Is this what you're looking for, amorcito?

MACHO: Coño, who wears the pantalones around here, anyway!

CHISMOSA: (CHISMOSA *and* BRUJA *take off their skirts, revealing black leather pants studded with spikes.*) You mean these, sugah?

VÍBORA: ¡En la madre!

BRUJA: (*With a whip, a la S&M.*) ¡Tu padre!

COYOTE: Anoint thee, Bruja!

MACHO: Bitches! We'll have you turning tricks twenty-four hours per day.

VÍBORA: (*As the men try to get him into the fray.*) ¡Si no me van a coger, no me molesten! (*Choreographed dance scene.* LAS MUJERES *soundly trash the men who grovel on the floor.*)

MACHO: Okay. All right, ya basta, you won, uncle, uncle! ¡Tío! ¡Tío!

COYOTE: My, grandma, what big teeth you have!

VÍBORA: No me toquen, no me toquen ... ¡que me dan cosquillas! (LAS MUJERES *manacle and chain the men who are down on all fours.*)

BRUJA: ¡Ahora, sí, el nuevo orden! (*To* COYOTE.) Lick my boots, swine!

CHISMOSA: ¡A cortarles los cojones a todos! (MACHO *holds on to his testicles and shrieks.*)

VÍBORA: Well, I don't care.

BRUJA: Now then, you studs, shall we sing in castrato?

DIABLOS: ¡Ay, ay, ay, ay! Canta y no llores ...

BRUJA AND CHISMOSA: Las Mujeres run it! ¡Las Mujeres rifan! ¡Que vivan las Mujeres! (*Forcing the men to reply.*)

DIABLOS: ¡Que vivan! ¡Que revivan! ¡Que vivan otra vez!

NOCHE BUENA: (*Aside.*) It is here I make my exit. (*She leaves. Enter* MARIACHI.)

MARIACHI: (*Cumbia.*)

> He swam 'cross the Rio Grande
> Wanting to go to America
> But he met a long tall Texican
> Who told him "Go back, you Mexican!"
>
> He gave a man all his money
> for the land of milk and honey

They put him in a car trunk
Which put him in a blue funk

Passing by a mortuary
It hit him—"In death men pay!"
In life one thing is certain
I'll charge to draw their final curtain

I'll build them a house of death
Tombstones for sale or lease
Let your fingers do the walking
At Pancho's Palacio you rest in peace

CHORUS:

He went to Carolina for to pick tabacoo
He didn't get richer he just got more flaco

Went to California to pick grapes and melon
They put him in jail as a convicted felon

In Tulsa had to wash about a dozen plates
His poor health—deteriorates

In Dallas went to work in a Go-Go bar

He didn't—have a Green Card

(*Exit* MARIACHI. *Enter* PANCHO *in a black Zoot Suit, visibly more "human" looking. Enter* HOMBRE *and* MUJER *customers.*)

PANCHO: Just look at this beautiful cactus coffin in Aztec motif. And inside—mira! An American and a Mexican flag. Why, it even has a tape deck. (*He presses a button that plays "La Cucaracha."*)
HOMBRE: I love it. I would just die to be burried in something like that!
MUJER: Well, dear, yo no sé ...
PANCHO: You get a life-time guarantee on the consecrated ground.
MUJER: But this is so very expensive and we are very poor.
PANCHO: We give perpetual care for the life of the coffin.
MUJER: Haven't you got something more economical?
PANCHO: Bueno, we do have that—humble Farmworker model in the back.
HOMBRE: That lettuce crate!
PANCHO: Yeah, it's called "El Cheapo Special."

HOMBRE: I like this one much better.

PANCHO: Why don't you try it on for size!

MUJER: (*As* HOMBRE *jumps into the coffin.*) No, honey, vámonos. (PANCHO *slams the lid on the man behind his wife's back, killing him instantly.*)

HOMBRE: Ahhhhhhhh!

PANCHO: (*Restraining the wife.*) Ah ... sorry, too late ... once you try it on ... no refunds! Now, what'll it be, cash or charge? (*Mourners come to console the widow.*) There, there, there, don't you worry about a thing. Now, we have a special today and today only on Professional Mourners. We have those who cry soft, those who shriek and those who get hysterical and pass out. Rosaries are extra. (*The widow exits.*) We all have to go sometime! Hey lady, call us when you're ready! (*Counting his money.*) Stupid people!

VOICE: Hey, Pancho!

PANCHO: Who's that?

VOICE: It's me ... your conscience.

PANCHO: My conscience? Since when do I need a conscience?

VOICE: Since you gave up your horns and tail and moved to Houston. (*Beat.*) Why Houston, anyway?

PANCHO: It reminds me of home, hot and steamy.

VOICE: I thought so. You see, you really haven't left, you just brought hell with you!

PANCHO: Hey, I don't need you. I've got everything I want—money, power, viejas.

VOICE: Exactly, nothing has changed. Tell me, how much do you charge for a funeral?

PANCHO: It all depends. A Mariachi High Mass with a Mayan altar and stela costs un chingo.

VOICE: Ya ves, you may be burying the dead, but you're bleeding the living.

PANCHO: You expect me to feel sorry for those people! What did they ever do for me?

VOICE: What about your undocumented workers—how much do you pay them?

PANCHO: The mojados? Why, uh, as little as possible.

VOICE: You drink their blood! And you swam the river just like them.

PANCHO: Yes, but I pulled myself up by my bootstraps. This is a dog-eat-dog business. I have to lower my costs. The competition will cut my throat.

VOICE: Cut your throat, eh? You said it, Pancho, you said it. (*Starting to fade.*)

PANCHO: Hey! Who the hell do you think you are?!

VOICE: I told you ... I'm your conscience ... It comes with the baggage ... (*Fading fast.*)

PANCHO: What baggage?

VOICE: Being ... human. (*Fades completely.*)

PANCHO: Human! Oh no! I hate humans! They make me sick! (*He leans against a coffin.*)

> How very sad is man's condition
> he lives on earth a mere rendition
> of what befalls him when he dies—
> and falls into the veil of woes and lies.

(*The coffin opens up. Out pops* JESÚS.)

JESÚS: ¡Ay-ay-ay! Perdóname, señor, I didn't mean to disturb you.

PANCHO: Who are you—what are you doing in there?

JESÚS: Allow me to introduce myself, soy Jesús Domingo, para servirle.

PANCHO: Jesús ... Sunday? (*Taking a good look at him.*) Are you my conscience?

JESÚS: No, señor, I am only a poor soul looking for a place to rest my weary bones.

PANCHO: Looks like you got shot.

JESÚS: In Houston the cops shoot first and ask questions later— especially if you're Mexicano.

PANCHO: Why didn't you go to El Cielito Lindo?

JESÚS: They wouldn't issue me a visa. So, I had to go to El Infierno. When I got there it was closed.

PANCHO: Closed? La Gran Cantina del Infierno, closed! Are you jiving me?

JESÚS: No, you should have seen the line of people waiting to get in. There was a roadblock patrolled by Amazons in leather and whips and a big sign that said, "Abandon All Esperanza of Entering Aquí."

PANCHO: ¡Maldita sea mi estampa!

JESÚS: So, I had to go back across the Río ... Styx.

PANCHO: The oarsman, Charro, did he charge you another fare?

JESÚS: Yes, in dollars. I see you came as an espalda mojada. You know, a wetback. (*Pointing to* PANCHO'*s back.*)

PANCHO: Wetback ...

JESÚS: Strange about that dirty river. Once you get wet, you stay wet for life.

PANCHO: You know, we're all wetbacks here. Yeah. Some people swam an ocean to get to the promised land. Now, Geeesusssss, let me get this straight ...

JESÚS: No, sir, it's Jesús Domingo.

PANCHO: I see it now!

JESÚS: What?

PANCHO: Man's inhumanity to man! God, what a horrible condition! What are you going to do?

JESÚS: I want to plead my case before our Holy Father, El Papa. You see, I was on my way to confession when the cops shot me.

PANCHO: Christ almighty! He can't help you.

JESÚS: The last name is Domingo, Señor.

PANCHO: What kind of cops were they?

JESÚS: Border Patrol!

PANCHO: God's Border Patrol?

JESÚS: It's not fair. Sure, I was what they called an "illegal alien." But I worked hard all my life. I paid my taxes and never collected welfare or food stamps.

PANCHO: I see it all now! My conscience was right! I renounce my wealth! (*Going down on his knees.*) From now on, I'm going to work for the good of mankind.

JESÚS: Great, you can start with me. I need help to get to heaven.

PANCHO: No, Jesús, you don't want to go to heaven. It's gotten real discriminatory up there. They only admit a certain class of people. Or else you have to belong to a "special club."

JESÚS: How do you know so much about this place?

PANCHO: Jesús! I used to work up there! I was as close to God as anybody!

JESÚS: Really!

PANCHO: We all have the capacity to be God! Yes, you, me, everyone! That's it, that's it! That's the answer. (*Screaming up to heaven.*) I wasn't at fault! You were! You egomaniac!

JESÚS: Calm down. Calm down!

PANCHO: I was not to blame! I was not to blame! Oh God, it's taken me all these years to realize that! Oh Jesús Christ!

JESÚS: Jesús Domingo ...

PANCHO: Look, here's what we're going to do. We're going to create our own paradise right here on earth!

JESÚS: But how?

PANCHO: Not with a bullet, not with a ballot, but with a Bible! (*Pulls out a Bible.*)

JESÚS: A Bible?

PANCHO: And this! (*Pulling out a microphone.*) Come, you must go forth and recruit an army of lost souls like us, to build the Kingdom of Heaven on Earth. (*They exit.*)

MACHO: (*Entering from the wings with the other* DIABLOS.) Man, am I glad to get away from las mujeres.

COYOTE: Pinches bull dykes.

MACHO: If only Pancho hadn't quit.

VÍBORA: Well, let's go find the cabrón. I kind of miss him, anyway. Nobody could wield a whip like that man.

MACHO: Which way?

COYOTE: Just follow the stench.

VÍBORA: Yuck! I think they're burning up the ozone layer. (*Exit* DIABLOS. *Blinding lights up on El Cielito Lindo.* DIOS, *a Chicano with a magnificent Zapata-mustache is seated on a white wicker chair smoking a Cuban cigar and talking to* SAN PEDRO.)

SAN PEDRO: . . . so the line of lost souls is backed clear to infinity. Live people are scared of death. They're blaming this wave of illegals on a Nicaraguan-Cuban-Soviet conspiracy.

DIOS: How's the Diablo?

SAN PEDRO: He's in a desolate place called Houston . . . in the state of turmoil . . . no, Texas. Fabulously wealthy, nouveau riche, owns ten low rider Rolls Royces, beautiful women, you name it.

DIOS: Ay, qué maldito, almost makes me jealous.

SAN PEDRO: We have to stop him now. People think it's the end of the world.

DIOS: Well, I think this is a job for Super-Chuy!

SAN PEDRO: Your son?

DIOS: My one and only. Where is the boy?

SAN PEDRO: I don't know, I haven't seen him since Resurrection Sunday.

DIOS: Have Gabriel blow his horn to summon him hither. (*Trumpet blows in the distance.*) By the by, how are the souls judged fit to enter the Kingdom of Heaven?

SAN PEDRO: Oh, no problem with them. Of course, we only get five or six per week. Traffic is kind of light up this way.

DIOS: Care for a cigar? It's Cuban . . . one of my finest creations.

SAN PEDRO: No, thank you. They say smoking is bad for your health.

DIOS: Balderdash! I've been smoking for millions of years. (*He starts coughing.*) Never did me ... any ... harm.

SAN PEDRO: Lord, if you pardon my saying so, your son hasn't gotten over the trauma.

DIOS: What trauma?

SAN PEDRO: You know, Calvary, the Via Dolorosa, the whole bit.

DIOS: Nonsense. He got great reviews! The Bible is the best seller of all time. But that's water over the dam. They love him now. He plays in all the best houses! (*Enter* CHUY.) Ahhhh, here he is.

CHUY: Quiubole, Pop.

DIOS: My boy! Let me take a good look at you. (*To* SAN PEDRO.) Spitting image of his Dad. ¿Cómo estás, m'ijo?

CHUY: Bien, just hanging in there. (CHUY *carries a cross on his back.*)

DIOS: Still bearing your cross, eh? How's your Mamacita?

CHUY: Fine, she's living in Mexico City. They made her la Virgen de Guadalupe, you know.

DIOS: Ah, yes, those Mexicanos sure love their Mamasotas. Well now, let's talk turkey. The Diablo has quit his job and gone to earth to raise hell.

CHUY: I knew he'd get fed up sooner or later.

SAN PEDRO: The system has gone helter-skelter.

DIOS: That's it in a nutshell, my boy. How'd you like to take another crack at it?

CHUY: (*Showing them the holes in his hands.*) Pops, look at these holes in my hands!

SAN PEDRO: (*To* DIOS.) What did I tell you?

DIOS: Are you denying me, your Father?

CHUY: No, Señor, it's just that people are such ...

DIOS: Go on, say it!

CHUY: ¡Cabrones!

SAN PEDRO: Scandalous!

DIOS: Explain yourself!

CHUY:

The People are Such Cabrones (*Rap.*)

People just haven't learned
no they just haven't learned
put a saint among their midst
and they'll chop him into bits

Dig, if I would appear

on that planet so dear
they would think it was a hoax
they would treat it as a joke

Or else they would say
he's not Cristo, oh no way
they would think I was from Mars
or an alien from the stars

DIOS: (*Sings.*)

But they need you right now
yes they need you so much
come on, take another change
prove you have the magic touch

CHUY:

Dad, please listen to me
I will tell you once more
miracles are so passé
they themselves must make their day

DIOS: (*To* SAN PEDRO.)

Have you ever heard such prattle!

CHUY:

Ah, the truth has got you rattled!

Pop, with all due respect
your memory's gone defect

DIOS:

Oh, what's that you say
I can't hear you no way

CHUY:

Why can't you send Gabriel
or, San Pedro, they're able

DIOS:

They are getting on in years
they are growing old, I fear
Pete's sword has gone rusty
Gabe's horn's not so lusty

SAN PEDRO: (*To* CHUY.)

You're the one with the track record.

CHUY:

My results were very checkered.

DIOS:

So, have you had your say?

CHUY:

I can't go, oh no way.

DIOS:

Then I'll have to send someone
who's a bigger son-of-a-gun.

SAN PEDRO:

Well now, who could that be?

DIOS:

What would you say to me?

(*Blackout on heaven. Down on earth the* POPE *appears, talking on
the telephone. An answering machine responds with the
following recording.*)

DIOS: (*Voice.*) ¡Hola! This is Dios. Gracias for calling. I am not
available at the moment, but if you would please leave
me your name, number, and a message, I promise to get
back to you as soon as I can. Wait for the beep, y ahí te
watcho! (*Beep.*)

POPE: Hell-lo-a, hell-lo-a. Dis is a Pope Papa. Operator, don't
you have any other listings for God, da Father?

OPERATOR: (*Voice.*) I'm sorry, sir, all His other lines are busy.

POPE: All righta, thena lemme talka to Jesu Cristus.

OPERATOR: I'm sorry, sir, His phone has been disconnected.

POPE: ¿La Virgen María?

OPERATOR: She has an unlisted number. Thank you for using
A.T. and T.

POPE: Waita minute! This is an emergency. I'll talka to anybody!

SAN PEDRO: (*Appearing on high.*) Pearly Gate Control Tower,
San Pedro here.

POPE: Pete! Pete, my boy, is thata you?

SAN PEDRO: Pope Papa! Long time no see.

POPE: Thatsa me, the Holy See! Listen, Pete, we ina big trouble.

SAN PEDRO: ¿Qué pasó? You still trying to get the choir boys to see forever in alto?

POPE: No, no, no! Listen, all the dead people is coming back. You know, we put 'em in, they poppa out. All kinds of crazy signs, Pete. Acid rain, Star Wars, Nancy Reagan. Just like the Booka Revelations. Peter, I fear the World War Número Three ...

SAN PEDRO: ... strikes and you're out! I might as well level with you. It is the Second Coming!

POPE: Mama mía!

SAN PEDRO: So, you better get rid of that Villa and the mistress.

POPE: Of course, I'm celebate, celebate. I'll say a High Mass, write a Papul Bull. But wait, who is a coming. He is a coming? Does he have hotel reservations? Does he need a rented car?

SAN PEDRO: Dios, el Padre ...

POPE: Oh no? Not the Son, not the Ghost?

SAN PEDRO: The Big Guy.

POPE: The one who goes by Old Testament Rules?

SAN PEDRO: Mr. Law and Order.

POPE: Who hides out in burning bushes?

SAN PEDRO: Who wrote the "Ten Commandments" for Charlton Heston?

POPE: Pete! Don't hang up. What does he look like? Where will he land?

SAN PEDRO: He will be disguised, but you will know him by his deeds! (*The phone goes dead. Blackout.*)

ACT TWO

A long rope hangs from the rafters. Down it slides a fat BORDER PATROL MAN *dressed in boots, spurs, cowboy hat, shades, and a glowing "red neck."*

BORDER PATROL:

> Los ojos de Tejas are watchándote
> todo el live long día
> los ojos de Tejas are watchándote

a ti y a tu tía
Watcha la migra no te cache
oh, so early en el día
watcha la migra no te cache
a ti y a tu tía
(*Letting out a "grito" and making the "hook 'em horns"
sign.*)
Hook 'em horns!

(BORDER PATROL *enters the "Goodnight Lounge" with* MARY
GOODNIGHT *behind the counter.* GOODNIGHT *wears a blonde
wig with layers of white make-up on her face.*)

GOODNIGHT: What'll it be, stranger?

BORDER PATROL: Gimme a beer, Lone Star.

GOODNIGHT: Coming right up, cowboy.

BORDER PATROL: Beg'n yore pardun, ma'am, but I ain't no or-
　　　dinary cowboy. I'm an Immigration and Naturalization
　　　Service Agent.

GOODNIGHT: Well, sit yourself down and wet your whiskers. I'm
　　　Mary Goodnight, owner of this here "Goodnight Lounge."

BORDER PATROL: I'm what you people called the "migra."

GOODNIGHT: What do you mean, "you people?"

BORDER PATROL: Your people, the Meskins. Don't you call
　　　Border Patrol Agents "la migra."

GOODNIGHT: I ain't Meskin.

BORDER PATROL: Excuse me, ma'am, I didn't mean to insult
　　　you.

GOODNIGHT: You got your nerve, coming in here and calling
　　　me a Meskin.

BORDER PATROL: I'm truly sorry, little lady, I thought this here
　　　was a Meskin bar-ee-oo.

GOODNIGHT: This *is* a Meskin Bar-ee-oo, but not everyone is
　　　Meskin. Does "Mary Goodnight" sound like a Mexican
　　　name to you?

BORDER PATROL: No, but ...

GOODNIGHT: But what?

BORDER PATROL: What are you?

GOODNIGHT: I'm 100 per cent 'Merican and proud of it.

BORDER PATROL: Then how come ...

GOODNIGHT: What?

BORDER PATROL: You're so prieta ...

GOODNIGHT: I don't understand Spanish. What are you doing
　　　here, gordo?

BORDER PATROL: I'm here to catch me some illegal aliens. You got any working for you?

GOODNIGHT: Hell no! I wash my own dishes. And there's nothing I like better than to sweep and mop my own floor.

BORDER PATROL: Good. You know it's agin the law to hire them nasty rascals.

GOODNIGHT: Listen here, I do my own housework, my own cooking, even my own construction. And when I'm hungry, I go out to the fields and pick my own crops.

BORDER PATROL: That's the way I intended it to be! How 'bout your customers, any illegals among 'em?

GOODNIGHT: Landsakes, no! I card them at the door. Make them recite the Pledge of Allegiance in English.

BORDER PATROL: You're a good old gal, Mary. Gimme 'nuther Lone Star. You know it's getting so more people speak Spanish than 'Mcrican.

GOODNIGHT: Yup, I think we should change them Spanish names back into English.

BORDER PATROL: Yup, I agree. Tornillo, Texas would be Screw, Texas. And Amarillo should be Yellow, Texas.

GOODNIGHT: Yup. So, watcha doing 'round these here parts?

BORDER PATROL: Keep this under your hat ... er, bonnet ... er, beehive.

GOODNIGHT: This is mah hair! Don't you like it?

BORDER PATROL: Well, yup, sure. But is it your real hair? It ain't dyed or streaked or anything like that?

GOODNIGHT: No, I'm natural blonde. I come from a long line of Anglo-Saxon blondes.

BORDER PATROL: And you don't speak ... Spanish?

GOODNIGHT: No, English! So, what are you doing here?

BORDER PATROL: I'm looking for a hell raiser named Pancho Diablo.

GOODNIGHT: ¡Híjole!

BORDER PATROL: What you say?

GOODNIGHT: I said "hee-hoooo!"

BORDER PATROL: You know anybody by that name?

GOODNIGHT: No.

BORDER PATROL: Are you sure? This Pancho Diablo has a way of stealing into people's hearts and turning them upside down. Why, every ill this country suffers can be blamed squarely on his shoulders: drug addiction, unemployment, AIDS, the deficit, traffic jams, you name it. (*Air raid siren goes off.*) What was that?

GOODNIGHT: Air raid siren. Ain't you heard? We're in a state
    of red alert. The President says the Ruskies are behind
    this invasion of illegals.
BORDER PATROL: Well, that's why I'm here. To put things
    straight and regain control of our borders.
GOODNIGHT: Well, I'm glad. Have another Lone Star, on the
    house.
BORDER PATROL: Thanks. You know, María, you're a real purty
    gal.
GOODNIGHT: The name is "Mary."
BORDER PATROL: I like the way your cheekbones are so high,
    and your accent's so cute. Are you sure you ain't Latin?
GOODNIGHT: How many times I gotta tell yah! My name is
    Mary Goodnight. I'm owner of the Goodnight Lounge!
    And I'm Anglo!
BORDER PATROL: I didn't mean to rile you none, lady. It's just
    that you're as purty as a night in heaven, and the stars
    sparkle in your eyes.
GOODNIGHT: Ain't you getting kinda personal like? Just who
    the heck you think you are?
CHORUS:

> God's Country (*Country & Western.*)

> Well there ain't no grief in Texas
> and there ain't no crying here
> this is what they call God's Country
> with the pickups, oil and beer

BORDER PATROL:

> I'm a God fearing man
> who drives a Cadillac
> and you know that right from the start
> I really liked the way you are

> So just tell me darlin' gal
> the words I want to hear
> 'cause all I really need
> is to stay with you right here

MARY:

> I can see that you're not shy
> but don't get too many ideas

and if you're looking for a wife
do not try to find her here
But you keep talking like that
and buy up some more beer
maybe after a while
you will sweeten up my cars

CHORUS:

People fall in love
they all lose control
this is the magic land
of the Border Patrol
look at all the stars
in the sky above
you'll get mesmerized
and will fall in love

BORDER PATROL:

Well, I'm real glad I came
and I'm glad that I met you
'cause I'm sure that you also need
somebody to chase the blues
come on darlin' gal
get a little near
be my honey bun, be my sweetie bear

BORDER PATROL: Thanks a whole bunch, honey, you shore been a great big help.

GOODNIGHT: Wait a minute, where you going? Who are you? What's your name?

BORDER PATROL: Just call me Tex-Rex. (*Stepping down from barstool.*) Now, if'n you'll excuse me, I'll be going on patrol. (*He exits, tipping his stetson.*)

GOODNIGHT: What a man! (*Blackout.*)

JESÚS: (*Entering.*) ¡Hijole! I don't know where I'm going to find that Army of Lost Souls. (*He runs into the* DIABLOS.) Praise the Lord! (*Down on his knees.*) It's a miracle!

VÍBORA: (*Trying to position himself in front of* JESÚS.) Perfect, perfect! Don't move!

JESÚS: Brothers! Welcome to the house of Pancho Dios!

MACHO: Hey, man. You got a joint? Any wine? Spray paint?

COYOTE: (*To* MACHO.) He said "The House of Pancho?" (*To* JESÚS.) This Pancho, is he tall, lean and hungry looking, with Aztec bigotes?

JESÚS: The very same! Praise Pancho!

DIABLOS: Praise Pancho!

JESÚS: (*Passing out hymn books.*) Now, our job is to prep the crowds prior to Brother Pancho's sermon. Here are the hymns. Get people to sing along. (*To* VÍBORA, *who is still trying to score with* JESÚS.) Please, brother, can't you show a little modesty?

VÍBORA: Well, you know what they say, the devil finds work for idle hands.

COYOTE: Don't you worry about a thing, brotha, we have everything under control. I've been running Pancho's campaign since time immemorial.

JESÚS: (DIABLOS *pull out "Pancho for Pres" banners.*) What are you doing? Pancho's mission is strictly pastoral.

COYOTE: Come on, Geeeeeeee-suuuuuuuuss, grow up. Since when is religion purely spiritual? (*Enter* PANCHO. *The* DIABLOS *cheer.*)

PANCHO: (*Taking* JESÚS *aside.*) Who let these pendejos, er, brothers, in here?

JESÚS: Well, you told me to recruit an army of lost souls. Besides, they claim to know you.

PANCHO: Well, I suppose if I can persuade them to follow the fold, I can persuade anybody.

JESÚS: Charity begins at home. Let us sing, all together now. (*The* DIABLOS, *meanwhile, are bumming smokes, molesting the pretty women, etc.*)

JESÚS AND PANCHO: (JESÚS *and* PANCHO *lead the congregation in a hymn.* DIABLOS *sing hymn off-key.*)

> "Mano poderosa, que nos dio
> su santa luz (repeat)
> Es hora que sigamos el
> camino de la cruz" (repeat)

PANCHO: Hermanos y hermanas, welcome to Pancho's revival meeting. We are gathered here tonight in the spirit of the true Lord. My topic is "Peace Among Men."

MACHO: (*The* DIABLOS *snicker and hoot.* MACHO *turns to a female member of the audience.*) Ay, Mami, dame un "piece."

PANCHO: The Bible tells us to love our neighbors and to have compassion for our enemies. At one point it even tells us to turn the other cheek. But, do we have the strength to turn the other cheek?

VÍBORA: (*Mooning the audience.*) ¡Ay, sí! I'll turn it anyway you want it!

PANCHO: I ask you, when the landlord comes to jack up the rent and you have to take food out of the mouth of your children to pay—don't you, in effect, turn the other cheek?

DIABLOS: (*Hissing and booing.*) Fuck the landlord!

PANCHO: When your boss cuts your wages, or fires you and you don't do anything about it, what is that but turning the other cheek? When a policeman comes and beats you over the head, and you don't strike back, are you not turning the other cheek?

DIABLOS: (*Furious now.*) Kill'em! Chingazo time! ¡Muerte!

PANCHO: The advice of the gospel to turn the other cheek to an unjust aggressor is the showing of great moral force that leaves the assailant morally overcome and humiliated.

DIABLOS: (*Raising pandemonium.*) Booooooo! Noooooo! Kill! Kill!

PANCHO: When Annas was interrogating Jesús and a policeman slapped Him in the face, Christ turned to his tormentor and protested: "Why do you strike me?" In other words, Jesús spoke out, defended himself, demanded justice.

MACHO: Now you're talking bato!

PANCHO: I'm not saying commit suicide. I'm not saying follow the lambs to slaughter.

COYOTE: Never! Never!

PANCHO: There has to be another way ... another way ... that way is ... (PANCHO *starts to lose control. He gets dizzy. A little* DIABLO *puppet jumps up on his shoulder and starts whispering in his ear.*)

DIABLO PUPPET: Peace Through Strength ...

JESÚS: Brother Pancho, are you all right?

PANCHO: The way is ... Peace Through Strength.

DIABLO PUPPET: (*Whispering in his ear.*) It's correct, it's simple, it's Christian.

PANCHO: Peace Through Strength—it's so correct, so simple, so Christian. (*Getting his directions from* DIABLO PUPPET.) If your enemy has one gun ... you have two guns! If the Russians have a million nuclear missiles, we'll have two million nuclear missiles!

DIABLO PUPPET: Strength is Peace, Death is Life, Hate is Love!!

PANCHO: Only through Strength can we find Peace! Only through Death can we find Life. Only by Hating can we find Love!!! (DIABLOS *wildly applaud.*) And you know this is

true because God is on our side and it says so right here in
the Bible! And you believe everything I say—don't you,
don't you?!!

DIABLOS: All Hail Pancho! Long live Pancho Dios! Pancho
Dios!!!

PANCHO: Now then, go out into the world and do battle! Christian soldiers!! (DIABLOS *and* JESÚS *exit led by* PUPPET
DIABLO *as* PANCHO *collapses on the podium.*)

VOICE: (PANCHO's *conscience, as before.*) Nice speech, Pancho.

PANCHO: Not you again!

VOICE: You shouldn't have listened to that little diablo ...

PANCHO: I tried to change my tune, I really tried.

VOICE: It came out all twisted, Pancho. Now you've really given
those crazies the ammunition to self destruct.

PANCHO: I give up. I'm going back to La Cantina. I don't belong
here.

VOICE: Pancho, you're trying too hard. Forget about the world
out there; it's a mystery no one can solve. Try to come to
grips with yourself. Look for the tiny dios inside you.

PANCHO: A tiny dios ... inside ... me? (*Slow fade on* PANCHO.)

*Meanwhile, back at the lounge, the BORDER PATROL drags
himself in looking all bedraggled. MARY is behind the bar. Another
air raid siren sounds.*

GOODNIGHT: Lor-dee! You look like something the cat drug in.
Did you get your man?

BORDER PATROL: I got mugged! Gimme a beer.

GOODNIGHT: Sorry, I should have told you this was a rough
neighborhood.

BORDER PATROL: You ain't kidding. I got propositioned three
times by people whose sex I could not even recognize.
Then a junkie stabbed me with a rusty needle. This ain't
the way I remember this place! I hope I don't catch AIDS.

GOODNIGHT: Here, let me clean you up. (*Taking a washcloth to
his face.*)

BORDER PATROL: Everything's all twisted and turned around.

GOODNIGHT: Say, your neck is brown!

BORDER PATROL: So?

GOODNIGHT: I thought all Border Patrol Agents had "red" necks.
You're Mexican, ain't ya, Tex-Rex?

BORDER PATROL: All right, call me Tex-Mex. This is only a
disguise. But I'll tell you something—you ain't Anglo,
you're Mexican also.

GOODNIGHT: How can you tell?

BORDER PATROL: By the nopal on your forehead!

GOODNIGHT: (*Looking at a mirror.*) By the cactus on my forehead. Very funny. So, now that our little secrets are out
... who are you, really?

BORDER PATROL: God. Dios.

GOODNIGHT: Jesús Christ!

BORDER PATROL: No, the Father.

GOODNIGHT: Sure, and I'm the Virgen María. Do you know
how many stories I listen to all day in this lounge?

BORDER PATROL: Bien, don't believe me. Just gimme 'nuther
cerveza. Make it a Dos Equis.

GOODNIGHT: Getting "ethnic?" Say, Dios, why don't you create
a miracle? There's lots of smog today. Make it disappear.
Oh, and the traffic jams here in Houston are horrible. People get gridlocked and shoot pistols at one another. Give
us a rapid transit system.

BORDER PATROL: You want a miracle, huh? Okay. The air raid
sirens are going to come on right now. (*Sirens sound.*)

GOODNIGHT: Big deal, they've been going on all day.

BORDER PATROL: Mary, or may I call you María? The world
will come to an end in thirty minutes and only you can
save it. Switch on the radio. (GOODNIGHT *switches on
radio.*)

VOICE: We interrupt this program to bring you a special bulletin.
War has just been declared between the United States of
America and the Union of Soviet Socialist Republics!

GOODNIGHT: Oh, that's clever! How did you do that! (*She turns
the TV on.*)

VOICE: The President of the United States will now make an an-
nouncement. (*"Hail to the Chief" plays.*)

BORDER PATROL: Both sides just launched preemptive strikes.
We have exactly twenty-five minutes before contact is
made.

GOODNIGHT: Oh, Lawd, you are a riot!

BORDER PATROL: Shhhhhhh! Listen, it's your president.

VOICE (RONALD REAGAN): I am sorry to say that our Star
Wars Space Defense Shield was not one hundred per cent
effective. If it is any consolation to you, our own missiles, about one hundred thousand of them, will soon land
on Russian soil. I want you to know that Nancy and I
are praying for you and all your loved ones. We will,
of course, continue to function as a government from

deep within the Executive Command Center here in the heart of the beautiful Rocky Mountains ... (*Television explodes.*)

GOODNIGHT: What happened to him?

BORDER PATROL: Wayward missile entered through the air ducts and scored a direct hit.

GOODNIGHT: Too bad. He was a nice man. I voted for him. Say, how did you know all this! Are you really who you say you are!

BORDER PATROL: I told 'em not to mess around with the atom. They wouldn't listen to me. Hmmmmmmm, just like the apple in the jardín.

GOODNIGHT: Now just a minute, you can't let this happen! Billions of innocent people will die!

BORDER PATROL: Don't worry, María, the same thing happened with the dinosaurs. (*Sounding like Carl Sagan.*) In a few million years a stronger, more sensible life form will take root upon the planet and prosper. The cockroaches, perhaps, because of their unique ability to mutate genetically, could become the dominant life force.

GOODNIGHT: No, no, no! I don't want to be a cucaracha! Can't you stop this madness!!

BORDER PATROL: What for? The world is obviously a horrible place to live in. How could any self-respecting human organism stand it?

GOODNIGHT: You don't know where I was before! It was really hell! At least here there's hope, a promise of something better.

BORDER PATROL:

It Has to End Sometime (*Ballad.*)

It has to end sometime
might as well be now
although it was a nice
experiment ... anyhow

People are so weak
people are so sick
they want to end it all
let's do it fairly quick

GOODNIGHT:

But there's always hope
within the human breast
lies the milk of kindness
to bring out the best

BORDER PATROL:

Wars in every corner
children dying of hunger
polluted rivers and skies
why take it any longer

I gave man an atom
what did he use it for
did he make peace
no, he made war

GOODNIGHT:

Understand that we
survived many holocausts
to make this a better world
at any any cost

BORDER PATROL:

Wouldn't you be
happier with me
way up in the sky
up in God's eye

GOODNIGHT:

Someday I would
but stay here I should
there are so many things
I need yet to do

BORDER PATROL:

Like what?

GOODNIGHT:

Come to terms with me
understand who I am
find love with a man

BORDER PATROL: You've never been in love before?

GOODNIGHT: You think love was possible working in a cantina in "Boys Town?"

BORDER PATROL: You people are so ... sentimental. (*Yawning.*) Boy, being human sure is rough. Gimme 'nuther beer. I ain't been this sleepy in ages.

GOODNIGHT: Jeeez! Haven't you had enough. You drank seventeen cases already!

BORDER PATROL: Are you kidding? I can drink anybody under the table! (BORDER PATROL *passes out at the bar.* GOODNIGHT *tenderly wraps a zarape around him. Meanwhile, just outside,* JESÚS *and the* DIABLOS *appear.*)

MACHO: Oye, Coyote, did you like the way I firebombed that Taco Bell?

COYOTE: That's just what they get for defaming the gastronomic pride of La Raza. Did you ever eat one of their burritos? They're a sin.

VÍBORA: Look, I made a cold menudo bomb. Just leave one of these in their so-called Mexican restaurants and watch it explode. A slab of tripe in their puffy bourgeois faces is just what they need.

CHISMOSA: (*Entering with* BRUJA.) I don't see why we're chasing after those cabrones. Life was actually getting bearable down there.

BRUJA: Ironically, it can't work without them!

CHISMOSA: Oh, hell!

BRUJA: Good for nothing bums—think they can escape the fires of feminism!

CHISMOSA: ¡Ahí están los pinches putos!

MACHO: ¡Aguas! ¡Las viejas! (*They duck into the lounge, without the women being aware of it.*)

COYOTE: (*Pulling out a gun.*) Up against the wall, redneck mothers!

MACHO: One beer, two beers! Drinks on the house!

VÍBORA: What's this? A Border Patrol Porky Pig passed out in a state of bliss!

GOODNIGHT: (*Trying to wake up* BORDER PATROL.) You leave him alone! My friend is a little indisposed at the moment, so just go about your business.

VÍBORA: Look at this! A cauldron of menudo. Let's heat it up and boil him alive.

MACHO: Right, we'll make carnitas out of him.

DIABLOS: (*Dancing around the cauldron.*) ¡Carnitas! ¡Carnitas! ¡Carnitas!

GOODNIGHT: Wait a minute, please. Listen to me. You don't realize the seriousness of the situation. The world is about to be destroyed by a nuclear holocaust and only this man can save us!

JESÚS: Who cares? We're already dead. Besides, what's so special about this pig?

GOODNIGHT: He's Dios! This man is Dios-Almighty!

MACHO: Wonderful! We'll make chicharrones out of him and wash it down with tequila. Get it—Holy Communion!

BRUJA: Hahhhh haaaaaaa! Here's where you sops hang out!

PANCHO: (*Entering.*) Just what the hell's going on here!

GOODNIGHT: ¡Pancho!

PANCHO: ¡Noche Buena!

BORDER PATROL: (*Waking up.*) Can't a feller git a little shut-eye 'round here?

PANCHO: That voice! It's Dios!

BORDER PATROL: ¡Órale! I got you now, Diablo miserable!

GOODNIGHT: Don't fight! Don't fight! (BORDER PATROL *and* PANCHO *square off.* DIABLOS *help* PANCHO, *while* JESÚS *and* MARÍA *help* BORDER PATROL. MUJERES *stand back and watch.*)

MACHO: (*Thrusting a knife in* PANCHO's *hand.*) Stick him! Stick him!

COYOTE: (*Handing* PANCHO *a machine-gun.*) Boss, use this, it's more efficient.

PANCHO: I don't need these ...

BORDER PATROL: So, you come here to raise hell, eh?

PANCHO: I didn't mean to!

JESÚS: I see it all now! He's the anti-Christ!

COYOTE: ¡El mero-mero!

VÍBORA: Where's the all-forgiving Christian? Is this your only side, terrible father! Fire and brimstone, pain and punishment?

JESÚS: (*Handing* BORDER PATROL *a pistol.*) Here's your pistola, Señor!

COYOTE: Oh, a born-again Christian.

JESÚS: I don't appreciate being deceived.

PANCHO: I was sincere, believe me, Jesús!

GOODNIGHT: Please, you two, there's no need for this. You used to be good friends!

BRUJA: Ehhh, let them fight.

CHISMOSA: Mejor para nosotras.

MACHO: (*Pulling the trigger on the machine-gun, wounding* BOR-DER PATROL *in the behind.*) Come on, maricón! Shoot him! Shoot him!

BORDER PATROL: Ouch!

GOODNIGHT: (*To* DIABLOS.) If you think Dios is going to turn the other cheek—you've got another thing coming!

BORDER PATROL: ¡Maldito diablo! ¡Me lo vas a pagar! (BOR-DER PATROL *lunges for* PANCHO *and brings him down.* PANCHO *kicks* BORDER PATROL, *not wanting to fight, and runs for the door whereupon* BORDER PATROL *tackles* PANCHO *and gets on top.*) I got you now, Diablo!

PANCHO: I don't want to fight anymore.

BORDER PATROL: You're only saying that because I'm on top, cabrón.

GOODNIGHT: No, no, no! Stop this! It's gone far enough. (*Enter* POPE, *a long truncheon in hand. He runs towards the combatants and thrusts the truncheon squarely in* BOR-DER PATROL'*s back.*)

POPE: Vade retro Satanás! Satanás delenda est!!!!!!

BORDER PATROL: Youch! (*To* POPE *as* JESÚS *drags* POPE *off.*) Who's side are you on anyway? (BORDER PATROL *collapses, exhausted.* DIABLOS *take advantage of this to blast* BORDER PATROL *with automatic weapons, etc.* PANCHO *beats them off and tenderly cradles* BORDER PATROL'*s head in his lap.*)

PANCHO: Are you all right?

BORDER PATROL: Of course, nothing can hurt me.

PANCHO: Will you forgive me?

BORDER PATROL: Yes, of course.

PANCHO: All I ever wanted to be was ...

BORDER PATROL: Go on, say it.

PANCHO: Closer to thee!

BORDER PATROL: Oh, you poor diablo!

PANCHO: I loved you ... once.

BORDER PATROL: We were good friends ... weren't we? (*Trumpets blare. Heavenly choir. Enter* SAN PEDRO, HOLY GHOST, CHUY, *etc. Thinking that the* DIABLO *is hurting* DIOS, SAN PEDRO *unleashes the* HOLY GHOST *on* PANCHO.)

SAN PEDRO: In the name of the Father, the Son and the Holy Ghost! Satan begone! (*The* HOLY GHOST, *something concocted by a very clever lighting designer, falls like a*

vengeance upon PANCHO, *incinerating him.* PANCHO
*howls like a demon and falls, seemingly dead, at the apron
of the stage. The melee masks* BORDER PATROL's *transformation back to* DIOS.)

GOODNIGHT: Oh, my God, no! Pancho! Pancho!

POPE: (*Entering and throwing himself on* PANCHO *in grief.*) Oh,
no! It can't be! God is not dead! Resurrect! Resurrect!

SAN PEDRO: What are you doing?

POPE: Giving our Father the Last Rites.

SAN PEDRO: That's the Diablo.

POPE: I'm sorry, my, eh, eyesight must be failing.

SAN PEDRO: And you call yourself the Holy See.

POPE: (*Walking over to* VÍBORA.) Praise God! You're alive! (VÍ-
BORA *shakes him off.*) Oh, excuse me. (*Going from demon to demon.*)

DIOS: (*Entering and taking command.*) Well, lets wrap things up,
shall we?

CHUY: You were great, Pop! (*Entering behind him.*)

DIOS: Thanks, son.

GOODNIGHT: ¡Dios! The thermonuclear war!

SAN PEDRO: The missiles are in mid-air!

DIOS: Chuy, take care of it.

CHUY: (*Making a few passes with his hands.*) I already did. Me
ayudó el Holy Ghost. We took out the plutonium and junk
and stuffed them with chicharrones, condoms and marihuana. That'll give the warmongers something to think
about.

DIOS: Good boy. Now then, let's hold court to settle all these
complaints. Who's first?

SAN PEDRO: Las mujeres and los diablos of the Gran Cantina!

DIOS: Step forward.

BRUJA: There's just one thing I'd like to know—why are there no
women executives in heaven or hell?

COYOTE: You see, see! ¡Ven como son estas viejas!

DIOS: Wait a minute, she has a point there. I never thought about
it. Peter, do a study and form a commission.

SAN PEDRO: Sí, Señor.

CHISMOSA: Señor, we mujeres have suffered much at the hand
of these machos.

MACHO: Yeah, but once they put the pants on, ¡se volvieron más
hijas de la chingada!

DIOS: ¡Silencio! What's it going to take for y'all to live in har-
mony?

BRUJA: Equal pay for equal work and a split decision making role in La Gran Cantina.

COYOTE: All right, but just don't screw me like I screwed you!

CHISMOSA: And end to prostitution and pornography!

VÍBORA: Respect for those with different sexual preferences.

DIOS: (*To* MUJERES.) Will you take them back?

CHISMOSA: On condition that they share the housework and the care of the little diablitos.

MACHO: I'm not changing any diapers!

SAN PEDRO: Silence! Dios will render his decision!

DIOS: If there's going to be a Hell, it might as well be a more humane place to live in.

CHUY: That's true, Dad, most people end up there, anyway.

DIOS: Lower down the temperature. I hereby proclaim the Equal Rights Amendment of the Cosmos! ¡Que Viva la Reforma!

ALL: ¡Que Viva la Reforma! ¡Que Viva!

SAN PEDRO: Sir, next we have the Heavens vs. Jesús Domingo, alias Jesús Sunday, lost soul. Clauses 4.2 and 9.1 of the Celestial Penal Code: Inciting to Mayhem, Selling his Soul to the Diablo.

JESÚS: Forgive me, Dios, se me metió el diablo. What the devil said made sense to me, especially in view of all the injustice in this world.

POPE: We must render unto Reagan and the International Monetary Fund what is theirs.

JESÚS: No, do not give unto Reagan what belongs to Dios! What belongs to the children of Aztlán is theirs to keep!

POPE: See! He is most impertinent and unrepentant!

DIOS: Be evenhanded with thy rendering, Pope Papa, do as in Poland as you would do in El Salvador.

POPE: (*Aside.*) We'll be ruined.

DIOS: And take off those silly robes! This isn't the middle ages! (DIOS *rips the* POPE's *robe off, exposing his pink, silk underwear.*) Pete, take a memo. Let's find a better way to select the Popes. Ask Mother Teresa if she'll serve. If she's not available, get Walter Cronkite or Plácido Domingo.

SAN PEDRO: Right, chief.

DIOS: (*Referring to* PANCHO.) Now then, what are we going to do about this poor devil?

SAN PEDRO: Here we have the case of Satanás, alias La Serpiente, Lucifer, El Cucuy, Pancho Diablo. Crimes: Section One of the Celestial Penal Code: Conspiring to Overthrow the

Universe. He also violated the Mortician's Code of Ethics and other groserías too numerous to mention.

DIOS: Punishment?

SAN PEDRO: We recommend that Pancho Diablo be incinerated and his ashes deposited for all eternity in the maximum security facility on Pluto.

NOCHE BUENA: Dios, please, allow me a word on his behalf!

DIOS: Yes ...

NOCHE BUENA: You can't live without him!

SAN PEDRO: Blasphemy!

DIOS: Why not?

NOCHE BUENA: How will you know the difference between right and wrong?

DIOS: You have a point there. I'll resurrect him. I want to hear what the sun-of-a-gun has to say. (DIOS *resurrects* PAN-CHO.)

PANCHO: ¡Qué chingaos me pasó?

SAN PEDRO: Ya ves, profanity! The first thing that comes out of his mouth!

DIOS: Now then, Diablo, how do you plead?

PANCHO: Guilty ... but with extenuating circumstances.

DIOS: Now then, tell me what you feel—en tu corazón.

PANCHO:

It's Great to be Back (*Salsa.*)

It's great to be back
all in one piece
not burned to a cinder
down on your knees
what can I say ...
I had my day ...
it's time to return
it's time to be born

SAN PEDRO:

Don't you believe him
not one filthy word
Master of Lies
Prince of the Absurd
don't give him a inch ...
return him to singe ...
back down to the pit

forever to sit

PANCHO:

> Now just one minute
> I may have been bad
> but that had to stop
> I am reformed
> no longer deformed
> so give me a chance
> to try to reform

MARY:

> Excuse me, Señor
> may I speak out here
> he's not such a diablo
> nor is he a dear
> please can't you see
> all he wanted to be
> was a little bit better
> and closer to thee

PANCHO:

> To the members of the jury
> I am asking for perdón
> we need to ask the question
> do you have good corazón

SAN PEDRO:

> Don't listen to him, he's tricky
> don't listen to him, he's bad
> he is just trying to confuse you
> with that old Latino rap

DIOS:

> Oye, Pancho, let's be amigos
> I'm telling you, let's be friends
> we shouldn't be fighting forever
> after all 'twas the same endeavor

PANCHO:

Listen, God, I'm very grateful
that you'll give me such a chance
I prefer to dance right here
with my love Mary Goodnight

MARY: Excuse me, the name is María Noche Buena! (*Taking wig off.*) And I'm proud of it!

DIOS: (*To* PANCHO.) Let's do lunch sometime!

SAN PEDRO: Are you crazy?

CHUY: Right on! ¡¡Amor y paz!! (*Referring to both* DIOS *and* MARY'*s action.*)

SAN PEDRO: I'm warning you, he'll raise hell again some day!

DIOS: Don't worry, I'll keep an eye on him. All right. Is that it? Bueno, happy trails!

CHUY: (*Turning to go with* DIOS.) Keep on trucking!

MARÍA: ¡No Diosito! ¡No te vayas!

DIOS: Sorry, I really must go now. There are so many things to do, new planets to create, old worlds to check up on. (*Walking away. He stops.*) But I will leave you with this thought. Don't judge a book by its cover. Remember that the devil appeared as a preacher man. Another thing, he was an illegal alien, but I let him stay in God's Country. The world doesn't need any more borders. Tear the fences down! Why are people going hungry on that side of the line, when there is plenty for all over here?

MARÍA: ¡Dios! ¡Dios! You can't go yet!

DIOS: María? Why not?

NOCHE BUENA: There's so much more we need to learn from you. Diosito, you haven't been around in ages.

PANCHO: ¡Buena idea! Why don't you stick around, it'll be just like old times.

ALL: ¡Dios! ¡Dios! ¡Que se quede! ¡Que se quede!

DIOS: Oh really, Pete, you see how these people are! What's our schedule look like?

SAN PEDRO: Impossible! You're booked solid clear into the next century.

DIOS: Chuy, what do you think?

CHUY: Stick around, who knows, you might learn something.

DIOS: All right, if you and Pete promise to take care of things upstairs! I'll stay!

ALL: Yeaaaaaaahhhhhhhhhhh!

DIOS: Only one condition. I shall be disguised. I will walk among ye. But I could be anyone. Therefore, you must promise

to treat one another with respect.
Enter MARIACHI. *All sing finale.*

MARIACHI:

Who knows? (Samba)

So ends the story of El Diablo
whose name was Pancho don't you know
he came to earth not long ago
to change his life over all

Now he's as human as can be
the devil could be you or me
and for that matter so could Dios
walk anonymously among us

CHORUS:

Who knows who's right
who knows who's wrong
who knows what's up
who knows what's down
you'll find the answer in the eyes
of every person you surmise

MARIACHI:

Is heaven up, is hell down there
or is it simply everywhere
are Dios and Diablo really signs
or are they simply in our minds
God could be you, He could be me
so could the Devil be as we
journey our hectic frantic pace
in this the lively human race

CHORUS:

Who knows who's right
who knows who's wrong
who knows what's up
who knows what's down
you'll find the answer in the eyes
of every person you surmise

EL FIN